Fundamentals of Accounts Payable

MARY S. SCHAEFFER

ISBN: 0615958117
ISBN-13: 978-0615958118

TABLE OF CONTENTS

Preface

Unless you are satisfied with an accounts payable function that is expensive, inefficient, makes lots of duplicate and improper payments, permits fraud and is continually in hot water with state and federal regulators, it is critical that the foundation of the accounts payable department be as strong and impenetrable as possible. This is not as simple as you might think.

To create a solid foundation, best practices must be used and strong internal controls integrated throughout the function. For all that to happen, a good understanding of the fundamentals of the accounts payable function is required. That is the goal of this book and it is a lot more complicated than many realize.

Now many professionals reading this book will already know some of what's included. After all, we all know how to pay bills. For starters, there's a right way and a wrong way to handle the functions related to paying invoices. What's more, the function is changing thanks to technology, new frauds and increased regulatory requirements. So, while some of the fundamentals have stayed the same for many years, a lot has changed.

And, that's just the tip of the iceberg; there's a lot more to the accounts payable function than just paying bills (invoices). In most organizations, travel and entertainment expense reimbursements, the issuance of Form 1099s and 1042s, the reporting and remitting of unclaimed property, the monitoring of sales and use tax and the calculating and paying of use tax and more are handled in accounts payable.

One of the many interesting facets of the accounts payable process is the way everything is interconnected. For example by their very nature, best practices incorporate strong internal controls. Additionally, techniques used to thwart fraud will also do double duty and help prevent duplicate payments. Strong internal controls also tie into fraud prevention.

What this translates into in the book is the fact that certain recommendations will be repeated in several different areas of the book, depending on the topic under discussion. So, don't be surprised to see the same recommendation more than once as you work your way through the book.

The book begins with an explanation of some of the most very basic tenets of the accounts payable function, truly laying the foundation for the rest of the book. It then goes on to examined the master vendor file, because I believe strongly that vendors should be set up, before a purchase order is issued. In reality, this doesn't always happen, but for the purposes of establishing the strongest foundation, we cover master vendor file first.

The book then turns to practices for handling invoices, the very reason most organizations have an accounts payable department. This is an area that has undergone big changes in the last ten years as have the topics covered in the next few chapters: various payment mechanisms. The book takes an in-depth look at how checks, purchase cards and electronic payments are used in today's accounts payable function.

Once that foundation has been laid, the book turns its attention to operational issues that deserve attention. This is broken into two categories: those related to invoices and those related to payments. We take a look at some of the more common problems related to each of these important topics as well as solutions to the issues in question.

The issue of inaccurate payments and payment audits gets its own chapter. That's because it is a crucial issue, especially for those who wish to run a profitable organization, i.e. everyone. Although many organizations have made huge strides in minimizing duplicate and other improper payments, they continue to be an issue. What's more, some organizations stick their head in the sand and refuse to believe this is an issue. It is. Saying you never make a duplicate payment is like saying you never make a mistake. Ahh, if only that were true.

This is followed by a chapter on expense reimbursements. Handling employee travel expenses is a thankless task, but one that must be handled. While very large companies may have separate travel groups, most handle expense reimbursement requests in accounts payable. There are numerous issues associated with this task, and many overlook some of them.

The next few chapters focus on fraud, an ugly reality that virtually every organization has to face on several different fronts. Payment fraud by outsiders, occasionally by insiders and games employees sometimes play with their expense reports are all addressed along with timely solutions.

We would be remiss if we didn't devote some space to a topic I believe is often overlooked, that of the accounts payable policy and procedures manual. We've got a whole chapter full of advice on how to create a manual and keep it updated. We've also got suggestions on added values you can get from your manual.

We could probably have written several books on the regulatory issues affecting the payment function, but this is not the place for that. However, each of the relevant issues is explained so the reader will understand the basics of what is required and why these requirements are in place. Too often organizations assume something is optional when it rarely so.

Most people don't think of accounts payable as a function that can enhance productivity. This is unfortunate because there's a lot that can be done where accounts payable can make a difference. We devote three chapters to this issue, breaking the productivity enhancements into operational issues, payment productivity and enhancements that can have a direct and positive impact on the bottom line.

No discussion on accounts payable would be complete without looking at the other side of the coin, the vendors. That's why there is a whole chapter devoted to vendor relations. We believe that is an important, but often-overlooked component in the accounts payable equation.

We close with a brief look at where we see the accounts payable function going. There's been a lot of change in the last ten years and we don't expect to see the pace slowdown in the foreseeable future. We've got some hints on what you might expect.

CHAPTER 1
THE FOUNDATION OF THE ACCOUNTS PAYABLE FUNCTION

Accounts payable is a lot more complicated than many outsiders realize. The purpose of this chapter is to provide a framework for the rest of the discussion. In this chapter, we'll take a brief look at:

- Why accounts payable issues are so important

- The three-way match

- The basic documents used

- The basic payments tools and

- What happens when payments are made outside accounts payable

Why Accounts Payable Matters

From time to time, most people who work in accounts payable run into a know-it-all who demands to know "what's the big deal about accounts payable?" These folks think that an effective accounts payable process is one where someone sits at a desk and simply writes checks for any invoice that crosses their desk. As those who work in the function know only too well, this practice would be a recipe for disaster. Here's a look at what could go wrong should an organization be foolish enough to follow such a practice.

- Reason #10: The organization would end up paying many invoices twice. This is because some vendors send invoices twice as a matter of practice (e-mail and postal mail) while others only send that second invoice when a payment is late. Whatever the reason for the sending of the second invoice, an organization not employing best practices and strong internal controls would result in duplicate payments – which vendors rarely return unless asked.

- Reason #9: The organization would be hit with more fraud. Once crooks realized that the organization was paying whatever invoices came its way, the less than honest ones would start sending double and triple invoices and perhaps even some for goods and services not purchased.

- Reason #8: As long as the organization was not concerned about the bottom line (and virtually all are!) ignoring best practices would be fine. For duplicate invoices and other excess expenses come right off the bottom line impacting the profitability of the organization in a negative manner.

- Reason #7: When best practices are not followed, payments are typically delayed. This does not sit well with vendors. Typically, when payments are delayed, vendors have a difficult time getting a straight answer as to when they can expect their payments. None of this is conducive to strong relations and hence vendor relations tend to be damaged.

- Reason #6: While best practices result in an efficient accounts payable function, the reverse is true when best practices are ignored. The end result is that additional staff will be needed to handle the same amount of work.

- Reason #5: It will come as no surprise to those reading this to learn that inefficient processes lead to increased expense for the accounts payable function. This may come in the form of extra staff, lost early payment discounts or late fees.

• Reason #4: While most would like to forget about the Sarbanes-Oxley Act, those in the public arena don't have that luxury. Since best practices go hand-in-hand with strong internal controls, no public company can afford to ignore the issue of best practices. It should also be noted that some private companies are subject to the strictures of Sarbanes-Oxley either because their lenders demand it or a large customer will only do business with organizations that are S-Ox compliant.

• Reason #3: Often times, not employing best practices results in inaccurate information which trickles down to the financial statements resulting in inaccurate financial statements. This is a worst case scenario and one that every organization should strive to avoid. It can also mean being singled out by auditors (internal or external) for financial statement issues. This is not an area where most accounts payable departments have any interest in being mentioned and most strive to avoid it.

• Reason #2: Inaccurate financial statements and financial reporting can lead to trouble for executives relying on faulty financial information for business decisions. Use of best practices in the accounts payable arena can lead to improved forecasting, especially when it comes to cash flow.

• Reason #1: If everything discussed so far has not been enough to convince you that best practices are a necessity, consider the following. By not using best practices across the entire accounts payable function you could be courting trouble with the IRS and state taxing authorities. All are looking for funds to bolster their sagging coffers. For example, many believe that under reporting of income by independent contractors and other self-employed individuals is largely responsible for the tax gap. The attention on this issue is focused on the corporate world for sometimes questionable practices when it comes to 1099 reporting.

Along the same lines, many believe that only one-third of all organizations that should be reporting and remitting unclaimed property are actually doing so. The result is that many organizations are wide open for trouble in this regards. And, you don't have to go far to find a story bewailing online sales on the Internet and its impact on the states collection of sales and use tax.

Given these issues and others, it is imperative that all organizations look at their accounts payable function and employ as many best practices and strong internal controls as they can integrate across the entire cycle.

The Three–Way Match: The Foundation of the Payment Process

Most organizations require that the accounts payable processor match the PO with the receiving document and the invoice before making payment. This is referred to as the three-way match and is the basis for most accounts payable operations.

When there is a discrepancy the problem must be resolved before the payment is made. Of course, if the invoice is for less than the PO, many choose to make the payment and ignore the problem. You will hear reference to the three-way-match in many conversations about accounts payable.

The Basic Documents

In order to have a good understanding of the entire accounts payable process, we start with a discussion of the basics. Let's start at the beginning, taking a look at the documents used in accounts payable to make payments. They are:

The Purchase Order - Most transactions are initiated with a purchase order (PO) completed by the purchasing manager and sent to the supplier from whom goods are being purchased. It should contain all the details about the purchase as well as terms. For many in accounts payable, this is where the first problem arises. They either don't receive POs or when they do, it isn't filled out completely and they are forced to assume that the terms are the standard ones agreed to by both parties when the relationship is first set up.

Unfortunately, if the purchasing professional has made a special deal with the supplier including extended payment terms and they are not included on the purchase order, the odds are good they will be lost. Often these special terms are not reflected on the invoice, the purchasing executive forgets when he or she approves the invoice for payment, and the invoice then gets paid using the normal payment terms.

In an automated environment, it is too easy to click on the tab that says standard terms and conditions, without giving the matter too much thought.

The Receiving Document - This is the document included with the goods when they are received. Some refer to it as the packing slip. It contains a list of the goods included in the shipment. Typically, especially in a manufacturing environment, the goods are received on the receiving dock and logged in by the receiving staff. In more than a few instances the receiving staff simply marks off that the goods are received as documented on the packing slip without ever checking to make sure that the delivery matches what is on the slip.

It is imperative that each shipment be verified at the point of delivery to ensure proper payment. Once the goods have been taken into inventory it is almost impossible to verify whether or not a complete shipment was received. This is especially important in those industries where variances are permitted, for example those where 5-10% underage or overage is accepted.

The Invoice - Most in the industry believe that the invoice is the document that causes the most problems when it comes to payments. It is prepared by the supplier and sent to the customer to request payment. It is supposed to reflect the goods actually delivered although overages are not always allowed, the agreed to prices and the payment terms.

Many organizations require that the invoice be approved for payment before the accounts payable department can pay on it. Even after it is approved for payment and returned to accounts payable, the staff generally reviews it using the three-way match described below and checks to ensure it hasn't already been paid.

The Fourth Document: The Advance Shipping Notice

Sometimes referred to as the ASN or the advance ship notice, the advance shipping notice is the notification of pending deliveries. It is comparable to a packing list and is usually the first notification an organization gets that the delivery might not match what was on the purchase order.

Advance shipping notices are typically used in manufacturing or large distribution situations.

Check Request Form

Not every payment has an associated purchase order and/or receiving document associated with it. Some organizations allow the purchaser to simply mark an invoice "please pay" and send it along to accounts payable for processing. This is a rather sloppy practice that can lead to problems—namely duplicate payments and possible fraud.

These items are typically referred to as non-purchase order items and can account for a significant part of an organization's payments. Hence it is important to have a good procedure in place to deal with these items.

A better practice is to require a check request form be filled out and the documentation, if any, attached to the form. If documentation isn't available at the point the check request is presented to accounts payable, it should be provided after the fact.

The form should have a place for an approval signature as well as the appropriate general ledger coding. Unless a check request form is required for every payment—and this typically only happens in smaller or specialized organizations—the check request form should not be permitted for invoices. By allowing a check request form to be used on an invoice, the chances of a duplicate payment increase.

Blanket Purchase Orders

When companies make the same purchase over and over again, say for office suppliers or rent payments, the need to complete a purchase order for each can create non-value add work. Some companies have taken to writing one purchase order to cover multiple purchases or payments. This is referred to as blanket POs and it generates a lot of controversy. Basically, it boils down to two schools of thought – people either love them or hate them.

If blanket purchase orders are used, care should be taken to make sure that they are not misused. At a minimum:

1) A dollar limit should be included. This can be an overall limit or a periodic limit, say $1,000 per month.

2) In the case of repetitive periodic payments, say for rent or equipment leasing, the blanket order should have an expiration date. More than one company has used a blanket purchase order to cover a lease and then continued to make the lease payments after the lease has expired and the equipment has been returned.

3) Blanket POs should be reviewed at least annually to make sure they are still relevant.

The Basic Payment Tools

Once you finish processing the documents discussed above, a payment is typically required. Let's take a look at the most common vehicles organizations use to make payments. They are:

Checks - The basic tool for invoice payment at most organizations is the paper check. Despite its widespread use, the paper check is fraught with problems. If the appropriate controls are not put in place, check fraud is very easy to perpetrate. Additionally, depending on the process, the actual production of the paper check can be costly and inefficient.

When one or more manual signatures are required, the time spent collating information, getting the signature, separating the backup, and stuffing the envelopes can be quite high. Additionally, if proper controls are not in place from the moment the check is printed through the time it is put in the mail, there is ample opportunity for crooks to filch checks.

P-cards - With all the problems associated with paper checks and the time involved processing small-dollar invoices, many organizations have turned to p-cards, also referred to as corporate procurement cards or purchasing cards. If distributed to staff these cards can have limits built in regulating the amount an employee is able to spend. The card can also have merchant category code restrictions built in to further control use of the card.

The cards have become increasingly popular in part due to the rebate most card issuers offer organizations using them. These rebates are based on volume with a minimum monthly dollar amount being required before the rebate can be earned.

In light of the productivity enhancements and the rebates earned many organizations look for ways to increase usage on the card.

Other cards - The most common card in many organizations, and for most a predecessor to the p-card, is the T&E card given to traveling employees. Some organizations mandate their use by their traveling employees while others recommend it but don't require it. Mandating use is one of the best ways to stop certain types of Travel and Entertainment fraud and is good for organizations to negotiate reduced rates with preferred carriers based on usage.

Fuel cards are used by those organizations with fleets as well as some of those whose employees' travel requires a good deal of fuel.

Then there is the one card that combines all types of corporate purchases on one card. The driving force behind the use of the one card is to get as much spend on a card as possible, in order to qualify for a larger rebate.

ACH Payments – Some also refer to these payments as direct payments. Similar to direct deposit of payroll, direct payments to vendors are made through the ACH. These electronic payments are inexpensive and result in the payees having good funds in their banks accounts the next day. An average ACH transaction might cost 18 cents. ACH payments can be either credits (the most common) or debits, depending on who initiates the payments.

With an ACH credit a payor directs its bank to take the funds out of its bank account and deposit them into the account of the payee. The most common types of ACH credit payments are direct deposit of Social Security payments and direct deposit of payroll.

With an ACH debit, the entity being paid directs its bank to take the money out of the payor's account and deposit into its bank account. In the consumer world this is typically used for mortgage payments or insurance payments. In the B2B world, this arrangement is not yet common. Some examples include:

- It is used by certain states for the payment of sales and use taxes, and

- Some oil companies deduct payments from local stations for goods provided and sold in their stores.

Wire transfers - This electronic transfer of funds is always initiated by the payor, which is very expensive, should result in good funds being in the recipient's bank account within a few hours after the wire transfer is authorized. It is typically only used for large-dollar transactions and the cost can be anywhere from a few dollars to as high as $50.

Today, organizations everywhere are starting to use the ACH mechanism to pay their vendors. Much of the activity that was previously handled through wire transfers has migrated to ACH.

Controls: Using More Than One Payment Type

When payments are made to any entity using more than one payment type the chances for a duplicate payment skyrocket. The best practice recommendation is that each vendor be paid using only one payment type and this be indicated in the master vendor file. To be fair, this best practice is not always possible to implement.

Controls should be put in place when using more than one payment type to ensure duplicate payments aren't made, POs and receivers are extinguished regardless of the payment methodology, and anyone making payments be trained with proper accounts payable best practices. Otherwise, as duplicate payment auditors will attest, duplicate payments will abound.

Many who work outside accounts payable think this is all there is to accounts payable. But it is just the tip of the iceberg. As you will see there's a lot more to running an efficient and effective accounts payable function. As you work your way through the rest of this volume, you will discover that there are many places the train can go off the track if proper attention and care are not paid to every detail of the payment process.

Payments Made Outside the Normal AP Process

In many organizations, wire transfers were often made outside of accounts payable. Since these tend to be large dollar payments, frequently for items where an invoice is not prepared, there were few problems. This is not to say that duplicate payments never get made; they occasionally were. And, when they did they were doozies. As we move forward into the electronic payment arena, it appears that ACH payments are more than occasionally being initiated outside accounts payable. This can present a real problem under certain circumstances. When a reader wrote to ask about payments made via journal entry, we decided to investigate the issue.

Recent research by Accounts Payable Now & Tomorrow reveals that at approximately 20% of all organizations, ACH payments are being made outside accounts payable. While this by itself is not problematic, what is troubling is that the staffs making these payments are not always given the same rigorous training that accounts payable staffs are.

This means that the focus on rigid coding standards, the requirement that purchase orders and receiving documents be extinguished and other standardized procedures are sometimes overlooked. When these practices are ignored the likelihood that a second invoice—should one appear—will be paid skyrockets.

To avoid this unfortunate outcome take one of the following steps:

> a)Insist the staff making the payments undergo the same rigorous training the folks in accounts payable have so that they don't unintentionally make errors that result in a duplicate payment or;

> b)Move the responsibility for all ACH payments to accounts payable.

Additionally, the following will also help.

1) Monthly review all wire transfer and journal entry activity to ensure no duplicate payment was made. These transactions should be compared to check runs and ACH payments. This review should be done for 60-90 days after the wire. If a duplicate is found, identify the internal control weakness that permitted this and fix it.

2) When the review is being conducted, associated PO and receiving documents should be extinguished (if they exist), if they were not when the payment was made.

3) Work with your auditors to convince management that normal payment processes should be followed when any payment is made, regardless who makes it. We're not saying that all payments must be made in accounts payable. However, if other areas making payments are not following best practices and including strong internal controls, a case can be made for moving that activity to AP.

4) Given the attractiveness of ACH pricing compared to wire transfer pricing, propose that wire transfers be replaced with ACH transactions, especially if they are handled in accounts payable. The savings can be substantial, if the organization makes a good number of wire transfer payments on a regular basis.

5) Have a duplicate payment audit performed by a third party contingency firm. If no duplicates or other erroneous payments were made, you are probably in good shape. However, if there were a large number of duplicates, immediately start an investigation into why they occurred and fix the controls that allowed this. Sometimes a report from a third party showing problems when payments are not all made by one department is all that is needed to get those other payments back into accounts payable.

As we move into the electronic payment arena in greater numbers, the challenges facing accounts payable are likely to grow. By recognizing where the problems might occur, you will be well positioned to deal with them effectively for your organization.

CHAPTER 2
MASTER VENDOR FILE:
WHERE THE PROCESS SHOULD BEGIN

The starting point for a lot of these issues is the Master Vendor File. It is sometimes called the vendor master file or simply the vendor file. The master vendor file is the repository of information for all vendors that the company does business with.

Not just any vendor should be able to get into your master vendor file. Before a vendor is entered, information should be checked verifying that the vendor is legitimate and that your organization intends to do business with it. Generally speaking, most organizations do not enter one-time vendors into their master vendor file.

The important point here is that the master vendor file is a repository of information for all the vendors that your company is doing business with. Maybe the word 'currently' should be added because you don't want a cluttered vendor file that has vendors in there that haven't been used for years and years. In this chapter we'll take a look at the issues around:

- Responsibility for the Master Vendor File
- Data in the Master Vendor File

- Naming Conventions
- Vendor contact information
- Controls around the Master Vendor File
- Vendor Portals

Responsibility for Master Vendor File

The question of where the responsibility for the master vendor file lie is frequently asked. Some feel accounts payable, others purchasing. This is an issue that could be battled forever. The correct answer is "it depends." It depends on where the appropriate segregation of duties can be maintained. If accounts payable can't accommodate the master vendor file responsibilities without maintaining appropriate segregation of duties, then the responsibility for the function needs to go elsewhere.

Typically it is sometimes put in accounts payable and sometimes purchasing. There is not a clear cut answer. For companies with smaller staffs in the function, appropriate segregation of duties can be a real concern. In those cases, responsibility is then sometimes moved to another area of the accounting department.

The Ownership Quandary: Three Questions to Ask Before Requesting Ownership

Are the master vendor file responsibilities handled outside accounts payable in your organization? Does this create needless delays in processing invoices because the person handling master vendor file updates doesn't take it as seriously as you would like? Do they consider updating the file a low priority task sometimes delaying the paying of new vendors?

If any of these conditions exist in your organization, you may be considering asking management to move the responsibility for the master vendor file to accounts payable. Normally, that is a strategy AP Now heartily recommends. However, before you go racing into your boss's office demanding the function be moved, take a moment to consider all the ramifications. Ask yourself the following questions.

1) Do you have adequate staff to assure appropriate segregation of duties? Regardless of the problems you may be experiencing, it is only appropriate to take on the master vendor file, if you can do it correctly. For starters, this means having someone work on it who does not:

    a) Process invoices,
    b) Approve invoices,
    c) Sign checks or
    d) Handle unclaimed property reporting.

2) Do you have adequate staff to handle the additional work that will be required, without it impacting your other work? Many times, the responsibility for the function will come without adding additional staff. If you suspect this is what will happen in your shop, make sure you have adequate staff to handle the task.

3) Are you inheriting a nightmare, either in terms of the file itself or the personnel associated with it? We're the first to admit, this is a hot-potato issue. But, this is definitely a case where a little up-front investigation is probably a good thing. You first want to determine if the group handling the master vendor file has been using best practices in its administration of the data or it's been an anything-goes-world. If it's the latter, you'll need to make a careful assessment of what's involved in getting the master vendor file in tip-top shape and if you have the resources to do so. If you don't, will management give you additional staff to take on the challenge? While we don't advocate walking away from a task just because a little hard work is involved, we do caution against inheriting another department's debacle and then getting blamed when something blows up.

The second issue is even more delicate. Will you inherit the current master vendor file staff with the function? If so, is the other department trying to dump its personnel problems at the same time? Again, you need to make a careful assessment of exactly what you are getting. By the way, there can be a silver lining in inheriting a person the other department views as difficult. The problem may have been with the manager and by treating your newly acquired employee with a little respect and dignity you could have a real gem who will be incredibly loyal and work hard to show his or her appreciation.

Master vendor file is an increasingly important function within any organization. Ideally, you'll want to have it in accounts payable, if at all feasible. However, if you can't handle it appropriately, better to leave it elsewhere. These questions will help you make that determination.

Data in the Master Vendor File

When it comes to entering data, every organization should have a rigid naming convention, a coding standard you might call it. It should conform to the conventions used when entering invoice data and for the creation of invoice numbers for invoices without invoice numbers. It should be rigid. Everybody should do it the same. It should be written down.

When it comes to entering data in the master vendor file, or handling any data for that matter, creativity is not an admirable trait. You want your employees to be creative when it comes to creating solutions, developing ways to attack problems, not when it comes to entering data.

Unfortunately in that instance, you need to be a little controlling. It may not be popular, but you need to say, "This is the way it's going to be done. Everybody needs to do it this way," and kind of a repetition of that old saying which most of us hate to hear, "Because I said so." Every one entering data must enter it exactly the same.

Keep in mind that once you start doing it a certain way if you decide to change it you really need to investigate what the impact of that change will be on data that's already entered.

Cleansing the Vendor File

Ideally, every organization should cleanse the master vendor file at least once a year. What this means is going through and identifying those vendors who you have not done business with in the last 12 or 14 or 18 months, whatever you think is appropriate for your business and deactivating them.

You don't want to delete them because if a vendor comes back and has a question about a payment or claims that they weren't paid, you want to have access to your records so you can respond to that inquiry, so deactivate the vendors.

Unfortunately, for those who have never cleansed the master vendor file, the first time they do it, it will not be a pretty job. The first time will take a lot longer than subsequent cleansings if you do it on a regular basis. Now, we talk about doing it once a year; some organizations do it quarterly. That's a great practice also.

Regrettably, what tends to happen with regards to cleansing the master vendor file is that people have good intentions and companies have good intentions, and then there's an emergency, a rush project. There's always a fire burning somewhere, and somehow cleansing the master vendor file gets pushed to the back of the deck. Then before you know it, it's three, four, or five years and you haven't done it. If at all possible, avoid that type of scenario.

Entering Data into The Master Vendor File

How do we get the data into the master vendor file? There has already been a discussion about limiting access to only one or two people who have the ability to put that information in, but where are they going to get it from? Some organizations have a vendor application that the vendor fills out. You might have a form that purchasing fills out.

Increasingly, we're seeing companies using a self-service approach for their vendors, for the on-boarding of vendors where they'll have some sort of an online form or an online portal where vendors can go and put their own information in. If you chose this route be aware that you will still need to assign personnel to validate the data entry. You are never going to get vendors to use the rigid coding standard that you want, but you can get them to put their data in, and that's another way to get that information in. It is a great starting point.

Needless to say, if the vendors enter their own data, they only have access to their vendor information. They cannot make changes to other vendors' data. Also, the only way they can have access is if the company sets them up with special access, typically requiring a user ID and password.

In the past, getting information into the master vendor file has been a hit or miss proposition. It's often not done completely. Many companies have been known just to take an invoice and use that to set up a vendor. Hopefully, the corporate world will get a little bit more formalized about their master vendor files as time goes on.

Naming Conventions

Sometimes naming conventions are referred to as coding standards. They should address every last possible issue that your processes might have when entering data. There's nothing too small or too miniscule about it. Even if something as simple as addresses, for example, if you think that street should be abbreviated ST. You may have somebody who thinks it's STR. There's nothing wrong with doing it either way as long as everybody does it the same.

A simple tip when you're trying to decide what to put in your standard, for address purposes use the standard set by the US Post Office.

More about the Naming Convention

There are many issues to address when creating your naming convention. Remember, for most items there is no right or wrong way. The important issue is that everyone enter the data using the same standard. Here are a few of the more common issues to consider.

- Issue #1: Punctuation. What do you do when there's a comma? John Jones, Jr or John Jones Jr.

- Issue #2: Spaces and Abbreviations. This is especially important. Spaces and abbreviations can create monster problems. What do you do for IBM? Does it go in as IBM, I B M? Does it go with International Business Machines? There are many varieties of that, as you can see. Decide what you think is best and then set it in stone for everyone entering information. Sometimes there's punctuation in a vendors' names. Do you include it? When you put Wendy's in for example, if you're doing business with the hamburger chain, do you put the apostrophe in? If you put it in and someone else doesn't put it in, it won't look like a match. You want to have a list of abbreviations. Again, do you put in corp.? Do you spell out corporation? Do you put Corp or Corp with a period after it? You want to address all these issues.

- Issue #3: The Doing-Business-As (DBA) Issue. You want to make sure you avoid DBA's. Insist on the use of the company's legal name.

- Issue #4: Leading Articles. When it comes to leading articles, do you include them or not? Do you put 'The Gap' in or do you put 'Gap' in? Again, there is no right or wrong way, just as long as everybody does it exactly the same.

- Issue #5: Individual's Names. When you put individual's names in, and you will if you're using independent contractors, consultants, you'll find that you have a number of them. Which do you put in first name: the first name or last name? Do you put in Mary Schaeffer or Schaeffer Mary? Again, there is no right or wrong way as long as everyone does it the same.

- Issue #6 Titles. Do you want to include titles? Mr., Ms., Dr., III, Jr., Sr. etc. What about professional designations after someone's name: CPA, PhD, and things like that. Also, what do you want to do with middle initials? Include them or not include them?

While it's not a definite best practice, it's probably a good idea to include them, especially in a large organization. When you have people with common names, sometimes middle initials are what can save you. It's not unusual to have two Jack Smiths, especially if you're a large company. Having the middle initial will help you distinguish one from the other.

• Issue #7: Industry Specific Issues. You also might want to consider any unique issues that you might have that are peculiar to your industry. The best one that comes to mind are vendors who change their name annually. You may be thinking, "What is she talking about change their name annually?" The one that comes to my mind is the US Tennis Open in New York. Its official name changes each year. One year it will be the 2013 US Tennis Open, and next year it will be the 2014 US Tennis Open. What do you do about that? How do you address that issue?

Vendor Contact Information

Most people don't give much thought to the contact information in their master vendor file. This is unfortunate. What's worse, is the contact information is often that of the sales person at your supplier. While this may be fine if you want to place another order, and that is what the sales person is hoping, the information is useless for most accounts payable inquiries. As you will see, it is critical that good contact information be maintained.

We've alluded to the need for good contact information because of some emerging issues that are going on and why we now have an additional challenge in accounts payable. Specifically, you need to be ready in case you are hit with ACH fraud, which you may refer to as electronic payment fraud.

The crooks involved in this generally are very sophisticated and their technology skills far exceed mine and probably many reading this today. Unfortunately, this puts a new onus on accounts payable.

When Contact Information Really Matters: Change of Bank Account Requests

When you get those change-of-bank account requests from your vendors or what looks to be like your vendors, you need to verify that these changes came from a legitimate party. To accomplish this, you need to have that good contact information in your master vendor file. The requests typically are coming by email, but they may come in a letter on company letterhead. Whichever way they come they look legitimate. I got one myself from what reported to be Chase Manhattan Bank. It looked like a legitimate email. The email even looked like it came from Chase Manhattan Bank. The only way I was sure it was a fraud was the fact that I don't have an account with Chase Manhattan bank.

When these requests arrive, you certainly can't respond to the email that was sent, and you certainly can't call the phone number that the supposed vendor has very considerately provided in the email. Because of course if you call that phone number or respond to the email, they're going to verify the faulty information. They're going to say that the change is a legitimate transaction.

Therefore you need to have that updated contact information somewhere, but ideally in the master vendor file, otherwise potentially, you will have a big problem.

How Good Is Your Contact Information?

Let's consider a few issues. When was the last time you cleansed your contact information in your master vendor file or wherever you have it? If you're like most of your peers reading this, your organization has never updated it. Most companies just don't do this. Now, we shared some statistics at the beginning of this course about changes and how often people change jobs. Consider this. How good do you think your contact information is?

Is there a better way? Ideally, when you first set up the vendor, get contact information, get the information for somebody in accounts receivable or treasury that you can call when you have a problem. Once this information is obtained, store it somewhere safe with ready access for all who might need it. One place might be in the master vendor file. If you don't have room there, you can keep it elsewhere, but keep it, and then regularly update that information. Now sometimes, people will say, "We're overloaded as it is. How do you think we're going to take that on? We can't take that on," and it is a legitimate issue.

But so is having ready access when you need it. There are now companies who outsource this. You can outsource this function and the outsourcer will collect this data for you.

The other approach that a small but growing number of companies are starting to use if to create an online portal or an online master vendor file where the vendor is responsible for inputting and updating the information. Perhaps once a quarter or once a year, you could send an email that says, "Has any of your information changed? If it has, please go to the vendor portal and update it." This is a simple approach that gets vendors to update their information.

Then, you've got the good information you need when you have to verify those phony requests that unfortunately have a way of trickling in.

The accounts payable function is changing. It's rapidly evolving. As you can see, from a lot of the stuff that we talked about with master vendor file, how we can treat our vendor data is changing. What we all need to do is make sure our practices are up to date, that we revamp them, that we continue to look at them and make sure that they meet the changing business requirements that we need.

Controls Around the Master Vendor File

For starters everyone needs to limit access to the master vendor file. This is both for updating the master vendor file and adding new vendors. Now too often what happens, is that the associates are processing invoices, and everything is going along fine, and then he/she looks to input an invoice and they can't find the vendor in the master vendor file. They say, "Wait a second. Hold on. I've got to enter this vendor in the master vendor file." They go ahead and update it. That is a poor way to handle this problem.

What that means is that anybody can go in and update, or anybody with processing access and that is not an appropriate segregation of duties. With segregation of duties, we want to have one person doing each leg of the transaction. That means somebody approving invoices, somebody entering them, someone entering data in the master vendor file, someone printing checks if you're paying by checks, and someone signing checks—all handled by different employees.

Sometimes, if you only have one or two people with access to the master vendor file, and they're taking vacations, they might be tempted to give their passwords to somebody else so they can do it in their absence. Resist that temptation. A much better strategy is to give that person their own password for the time in question while the original person is on vacation and then close off that access when the person comes back. Sharing passwords is just not a good idea.

Fraud through the Master Vendor File

Not all vendor fraud is external. We've mentioned fraud using the master vendor file several times now and you may be wondering how this can be done. Needless to say, your employees with larceny in their hearts can probably find more ways to play games than we can identify. We'll hone in on a few of the easier scams.

The most common vendor master file game is to simply submit a phony invoice (usually for a small dollar amount) for payment. If your controls are weak and someone approves the phony invoice because they are rushed, the vendor has then attained "legitimacy" and then future phony invoices, perhaps for larger dollar amounts, can slip through.

More devious employees have been known to hone in on inactive vendors that are still live in the master vendor file. They then submit an invoice under that vendor's name and address. Now, here comes the tricky part. Once the invoice has been approved for payment, the thieving employee goes into the master vendor file and changes the Remit To address to their own address or that of an accomplice. Once they have the check in hand, they go back to the master vendor file and change the Remit To address back to the original address.

These same tricks can be used to divert payments from a legitimate vendor to your dishonest employee.

The Master Vendor File Change Report

To guard against issues such as those discussed above as well as to just generally review master vendor file activity, a report of all changes to the master vendor file should be created on a very regular basis. Depending on the level of activity, this can be monthly, weekly or daily.

Someone should review this report, keeping an eye out for issues such as the one mentioned above. They should also look for any obvious errors or questionable entries.

In an ideal world this report would be reviewed by a very senior executive. The point of having a senior level person look at the report is to have the review serve as a deterrent. If it is widely known that the report is reviewed, employees may be less likely to try and play games.

The reality is that few, if any, senior level executives will have the time or inclination to review such a report. Thus the review should be assigned to a manager who will take the matter seriously. They should be encouraged to regularly question anything that doesn't look quite right, again so it is known the data is being reviewed.

Vendor Portals in Accounts Payable: What You Need to Know to Get Started

There's been a lot of discussion about portals in accounts payable in the last few years. That conversation has gotten louder in recent months and with good reason. Vendor portals (occasionally referred to as supplier portals) are just another step on the path to automation that is currently going on in accounts payable. But all portals are not the same. Let's take a look at some of the differences.

What Is a Vendor Portal?

Before we get started, let's start with a basic definition so we all are on the same page. A portal is an interactive, online repository of information that allows access to a variety of self-service applications. There are many types of portals and accounts payable isn't the only function taking advantage of them. Any time you sign up for free publications and then selected the different news alerts you'd like to receive you are using a type of portal.

In the accounts payable arena vendor portals are all the rage. It is important to understand that unlike the publishing world where anyone can sign up, vendor portals are by invitation only. It is not the kind of 'Open House' where anyone who finds your website can sign up. Your vendors should not be able to sign up unless you've sent them a link. Otherwise you'll end up with crooks signing themselves up to be your suppliers.

What Do Portals Do?

Portals basically collect information and allow self-service for many tasks that would normally require an interaction between the vendor and the customer. The most common example of a portal that replaces communication is the ones that allow vendors to sign into the portal and check on the payment status of open invoices. This keeps the where's-my-money calls out of accounts payable.

These can be stand-alone portals or part of a larger enterprise. Some readers may remember the development roughly a decade ago of interactive voice recognition (IVR) systems that allowed vendors to get this information over the phone. The IVRs were similar to the services offered by many pharmacies that allow you to call in and key in your prescription numbers for refills.

There are many different portals that can be used in accounts payable. For example, probably the most common portals are those used in connection with the electronic delivery of invoices either by a third party or directly by the vendors. In the case of a third party, it 'collects' invoices from a number of vendors and delivers them electronically to the customer.

Alternatively, a number of companies have set up portals allowing their vendors to deliver the invoices online by signing into the portal and uploading the documents or information. It should be noted that this is different than the simple emailing of invoices to an individual.

What Do Vendor Portals Do in AP?

Portals in use today in accounts payable cover a wide range. They can be very simple handling only one or two tasks to the more complex. Here are some examples of tasks handled in portals.

1) Delivery of invoices
2) Status of invoices
3) Status of payments
4) Automatic escalations of invoice approvals
5) Dispute resolution
6) Other vendor inquiries
7) Vendor setup for the master vendor file
8) Updates of information in the master vendor file
9) Track vendor diversity for government reporting
10) Track W-9 collection
11) Track W-9 verification using IRS TIN Matching

If at first glance this looks like it will replace most of the accounts payable department, we've overstated the case. What it will do is to remove a lot of the manual and clerical work handled in many accounts payable departments. But, these portals have to be used intelligently.

Let's take a look at the vendor setting itself up in the master vendor file. While the vendor can input its own information, care needs to be taken. If you just let vendors input their information directly, few will adhere to the rigid coding standard best-practice accounts payable functions insist on using. It's pointless to even try and get them to do that. What this means is after the vendor puts in its information; someone will have to review the information and change it, where appropriate, to conform to your coding standards.

So, while on some fronts portals definitely reduce work in accounts payable, they will create some new positions requiring a different set of skills. Portals are here and their benefits clear cut. It is imperative that organizations figure out what role they will play in the accounts payable function.

How Do You Get One?

There are two basic ways organizations get portals. They either purchase them or build them. Which approach your organization takes will depend on what the organization wants to do with it and how much customization will be required. If the organization has many unique requirements, the build-it-yourself approach might be called for. Alternatively, a third party model can be purchased and customized. That can get costly.

The approach most organizations are taking is to buy a pre-built model and if necessary, customize. Some of the models available are built so you can do a certain amount of customization as part of the basic price. From a cost standpoint, this is definitely a benefit. Also, a few of the models (especially the ones involved with electronic invoicing) are available on a SaaS or pay-as-you go basis.

There are a few models that shift the burden of payment from the customer to the vendor. This is not a good idea from a vendor relations standpoint. You'll occasionally hear a company bragging that their vendors don't mind paying. Really??? Typically this only works when there is an 800-pound gorilla in the relationship.

Expect to pay for the portals but also realize that after the portal is operational, your cost savings will exceed the expense involved in setting up and utilizing the portal on an ongoing basis.

Those interested in invoicing portals can start with the e-invoicing vendors. Go to their websites and sign up for an online demo. They are happy to give them. Some schedule these demos on a regular basis. Go to as many as you have time for and ask a lot of questions. Once you've narrowed your search, it's time for some serious discussion with the vendors in question.

How Vendor Portals Can Help the ACH Change of Bank Account Problem

As you are probably painfully aware, the crooks operating in the ACH fraud arena are very smart and understand how banking processes work even better than most professionals in the field. They've figured out a nifty way to get businesses to send them money simply by sending an e-mail or two. Let's take a look at how the fraud works, what you can do to prevent it and how the new vendor portals can help.

How The Fraud Works

First the crooks study your business and figure out who is making payments. This is an imprecise "art" so they don't always get it right. But, they often do. Once they have that important piece of information, they take a look at who your top vendors are likely to be. This is usually fairly easy to do. They may not be able to identify all your vendors, but they really only need one or two.

Once they have the two pieces of information needed to perpetrate the fraud, they prepare a simple e-mail purporting to come from the vendor in question. It tells its customer (that's you) that the vendor has changed back accounts and asks that all future funds be sent to a new back account. The number is provided.

These e-mails look legitimate. They may even include the logo of the company the crook is pretending to be. This is easy enough to get off most websites. In some cases, the e-mail address itself may even have been spoofed. So, simply verifying the e-mail came from the company is not enough. Nor is calling the company using the phone number provided in the e-mail, for if the e-mail is fraudulent, the phone number will be as well.

Detecting the Fraud

So, if you can't reply to the e-mail or use the phone number provided in the e-mail, how can you verify that the request is legitimate? The reality is that at the end of the day, most of these requests will be from your vendors. However, one wrong payment can make a serious dent in your organization's bottom line.

The best practice approach is to verify the request is legitimate by contacting the vendor using information you already have on hand. While at first glance this may seem easy enough, consider this. When was the last time you updated your vendor contact information? Regularly collecting and updating this information now has to be included in the work of any best practice accounts payable organization.

Using Vendor Portals

Vendor portals can help with this issue in more ways than you might imagine. For starters, most of the products on the market today are self-service models, meaning the vendors enter in their own information. This doesn't mean you won't have to do some verification after they've entered the data but it does cut down on the work being done by the folks managing the master vendor file function. The online portals do make it easier to both collect and update vendor contact information, which is needed from time to time.

There is another way vendor portals help with this specific issue. Since the vendor is responsible for input of all information, including change of bank account information, there is no need for an e-mail alerting you to a change.

The vendor simply signs into the portal and updates its banking information, if there is a change. With this approach, you never have to verify a change again. And, you don't have to worry about the change of account e-mails. You shouldn't get any legitimate ones taking this approach.

CHAPTER 3
INVOICE PROCESSING:
THE REASON ACCOUNTS PAYABLE EXISTS

The accounts payable function is handled very differently from organization to organization. Some handle 1099s in accounts payable, others elsewhere. The same can be said about just about every single issue discussed in this book. The one exception is invoices. Virtually every accounts payable function processes invoice. In this chapter we'll take a look at:

- How invoices were processed traditionally

- Electronic invoicing

- Handling invoices sent by e-mail

- Detecting duplicate invoices

- Handling invoices that are both mailed and e-mailed

Invoices the Old Way

Traditionally, a paper invoice arrived at the company and required a manual approval to be processed for payment. There was a quite debate over whether the invoice should go first to accounts payable to be logged in and then sent to the purchaser for approval or go to the purchaser first and only come to accounts payable after it had been approved for payment—and, theoretically, any disputes resolved.

While proponents of speedy processing strongly recommended the invoice come first to accounts payable that never became an accepted practice across the board. Regardless of where the invoice went first, there tended to be a lot of finger pointing over who had the invoice, when it was approved, when it was returned, and how long it had been sitting on someone's desk, whether in purchasing or accounts payable. The situation was definitely a recipe for disaster.

As you can imagine, the manual processes as described make it difficult to legitimately earn early payment discounts, those financial incentives offered by vendors to entice their customers to pay early. In fact, the desire to earn these lucrative discounts is what finally convinced some organizations to have invoices submitted to accounts payable first. In this way, invoices eligible for early payment discounting were fast tracked for approval and payment.

While this manual approach is still used in many organizations for a good portion of the invoices submitted for payment, there have been some technological advances that have smoothed the process.

A Word about Faxed Invoices

In the days of paper-only-invoices, making a payment from a faxed invoice was a really poor practice often resulting in a duplicate payment. Resultantly, many organizations had policies strictly forbidding paying from copies, be they faxed or otherwise.

This is no longer the case. Paying only from an original invoice these days doesn't offer the same control. The reason is that thanks to advances in technology, there can be many copies of an invoice that look like an original.

Electronic Invoicing

When companies talk about electronic invoicing, it's not always clear what they mean. The term encompasses many different delivery mechanisms. In the strictest sense of the term, e-invoicing refers to the automated process of sending or receiving an electronic document that is the invoice. Some insist it is an Internet based solution, although as you will see, this is not always the case.

In its simplest form, e-invoicing simply involves the emailing of an invoice, usually a pdf, to the recipient. However, and this is where the Internet part of the definition comes into question, there are some fax-to-email services available which permit the faxing of an invoice into an e-invoicing solution. Readers should be aware that some professionals do not consider e-mailed invoices to be e-invoicing. They exclude e-mailed invoices from that nomenclature.

Today, there are a number of quite attractive third party electronic invoicing options available. Some of these will handle small volumes of invoices as well as large. So, the belief that you have to have hundreds of thousands of invoices to make e-invoicing pay is no longer valid.

You may also hear the terms electronic billing, e-billing, or e-invoicing to refer to invoices delivered electronically either via e-mail or some other Internet-based mechanism.

Many of these electronic invoicing products are developed by third parties and have great features built into them, features that eliminate some of the problems inherent in manual paper processes.

When processed using e-mail, an audit trail is created showing when an invoice was sent. This effectively puts an end to the "I never got the invoice" game and proves when the invoice was returned approved for payment. The best of these models have an escalating approval feature designed to get invoices authorized for payment in a reasonable amount of time when the original approver is out of the office. It works equally as well should the original approver ignore the request for authorization.

Another great feature of some of the third-party systems is an online dispute resolution module, which allows communication with the vendor to resolve discrepancies quickly.

Self-Scanning

With the price of scanning equipment becoming ever more affordable in recent years, quite a few organizations undertook to scan invoices themselves. They could then treat these like invoices received via e-mail and forward them for approval and processing similar to those received electronically. This allowed them to accrue many of the benefits of a full-blown electronic invoicing structure.

Others set up e-fax facilities effectively converting faxed invoices into an electronic document without the invoice ever seeing the light of paper.

Accounts Payable Now & Tomorrow believes this is the wave of the future and within a short period of time most organizations will process invoices electronically, either receiving them that way originally or converting the paper invoices they receive to electronic documents. The benefits are simply too overwhelming not to take this route.

An Efficient Process for Handling Invoices Sent by e-Mail

Trying to stop vendors from sending invoices by e-mail is like trying to stop the water once the dam or levy has broken. Given the inevitability of e-mailed invoices, it is far better to develop an effective plan to take advantage of this new delivery method than to fight it. What follows is a rather simple seven-step process any organization can use to address the receipt of e-mailed invoices situation.

- Step 1: Recognize that you can't fight the proverbial City Hall and establish a formal policy for handling e-mailed invoices. This should be part of your formal policy and procedures manual for the accounts payable function.

- Step 2: Set up one e-mail address to receive invoices from suppliers. This should be part of your best practice strategy to receive all e-mails in one centralized location. Today that means one postal address, one e-mail address and one fax address. The e-mail address should not be a personal address but one that can be accessed by several people. This way, if someone is unexpectedly out of the office or leaves the company, there is no disruption to vendors e-mailing invoices.

• Step 3: Provide the email address established for the receipt of invoices to all suppliers. This can be done in both the Welcome Packet for new vendors and the annual letter to vendors. If you normally don't send an annual letter to vendors, you might send a special communication regarding this e-mail address.

• Step 4: Vendors should be informed that only invoices should be sent to this address. Nothing else sent to that address will be forwarded to other parties.

• Step 5: Vendors should be instructed not to send a second invoice by snail mail. Be aware that some will disregard this directive. Watch this process and create a list of vendors who always double submit despite your instructions. Paper invoices from these vendors should be discarded.

• Step 6: Different people should be assigned to monitor the account on different days. They can also fill in for each other when someone is out or on vacations.

• Step 7: Upon receipt of an invoice, it should immediately be reviewed and forwarded to the appropriate party for approval.

Typically, e-mailed invoices are first turned into a PDF and then sent to the customer. Great care needs to be taken that each is only processed once. For if you print the PDF, the hundredth printing will look just as good as the first one and you won't be able to tell which is the original and which is the copy. This means that routines for weeding out duplicates are more important than ever. It should also entail duplicate payment checking routines be integrated into the invoice processing function.

Invoices that are e-mailed are a reality every organization has to deal with. Trying to avoid the issue is not smart. Following a game plan, such as the one discussed above, is your best strategy for making this new approach work for your organization.

Mary S. Schaeffer

Three Simple Ways to Increase the Number of Invoices Received Electronically

The way we receive invoices has changed dramatically in the last few years. Just a few short years ago, emailed and faxed invoices were considered a royal pain by many. Today, most organizations are looking for ways to get vendors to send invoices electronically or by fax. As regular readers of this publication are aware, faxed invoices can easily be converted to emailed invoices by using relatively inexpensive e-fax services. What follows are three simple steps every organization can use to decrease the number of invoices received in paper format.

1) Let them know you are amenable to receiving invoices electronically. As amazing as it may seem, some vendors will not realize you are set up to receive invoices electronically. Let them know. You can include a one line notice about this on all remittance advices or you can send all vendors sending invoices through the postal service a letter telling them how to send you their invoices in ways other than the mail service. You might point out the benefits they will accrue by moving to electronic delivery.

2) Make it easy for those not using a third party system. Some vendors are not equipped or willing to participate in third party services. Provide them with a separate email address to use to send invoices. This might be something like invoices@abccompany.com or ap@abccompany.com. If you have an e-fax service don't forget to provide the fax number. If they are more comfortable faxing, let them.

3) Entice them by agreeing to pay them electronically if they invoice you electronically. This is an especially easy approach to use if you were looking to pay electronically anyway. You get two wins for the price of one effort.

If these strategies don't work, try mandating electronic delivery of invoices. But you'd better be the 800 pound gorilla in your space for this approach to work.

How can you take advantage of this new methodology in an organized manner? It's not that hard. Here's what we suggest:

- Set up a single e-mail address to be used exclusively for the receipt of invoices. Whoever is responsible for either processing the invoices that come into this address or forwarding them for approval should have the password, as should their backup and perhaps the department manager. The important thing is the e-mail account not belong to one person but several in case of absences etc.

- Set up a dedicated fax number to be used for accounts payable invoices only. Invoices can be retrieved throughout the day and integrated into the normal accounts payable workflow.

- Set up an e-fax facility to receive faxed invoices into an e-mail account. This should eliminate the problem of illegible invoices.

- Make sure your new e-mail address and fax number are included in all correspondence with vendors, especially your New Vendor Welcome kit.

- Convert as many vendor invoices as possible to this approach for delivering invoices. The benefits are overwhelming. Make sure you have management approval before starting the process,

Protecting Your Organization against Those Deadly Second Invoices

New invoice receipt practices have unfortunately resulted in quite a few vendors sending two copies of their invoices. Some are emailing them and snail mailing a hard copy, while others are mailing and faxing. Sometimes it seems that for every two steps forward we take, we then take one backwards.

Why This Creates a Problem

Second or duplicate invoices present a number of complications for the accounts payable department. Clearly there is the potential for duplicate payments, which are rarely returned without third-party prompting. Even in organizations with the best duplicate payment detection mechanisms there is a cost associated with these invoices.

The additional work created by the invoices adds to the expense of running an efficient department. Finally, there is the risk that an accidental second payment will alert a vendor to a weakness in your processes. At the end of the day, these second invoices mean:

1) More work for accounts payable
2) Potential for duplicate payment
3) The possibility of alerting vendor to potential for fraud

What You Can Do

We've seen a growing number of companies explicitly instructing their vendors on how to email and/or fax invoices. Included in those guidelines is the clear direction not to send the invoice more than once. This can be done politely with a "Please don't email and fax an invoice."
If that does not work and certain vendors continue to plague your accounts payable department with duplicate invoices, create a list of those vendors and double check all payments to them.

As always, utilizing accounts payable best practices will protect you against duplicate payments. Specifically:

1. Rely on the unique invoice number control in your accounting system. For this to work effectively it is critical that care be taken when invoice numbers are entered.

2. Extinguish POs and receiving Docs after a successful three-way match and payment has been scheduled.

3. Regularly check for duplicate payments and when you've recovered all the low-hanging fruit yourself, bring in a third-party contingency audit firm.

4. Pay all vendors on time so they have no excuse for sending a second invoice.

5. Consider automating the invoice processing using one of the third-party models currently available.

The second invoice problem is just one more example of how innovative accounts payable professionals have to be when dealing with the ever changing environment they work in.

This can be an honest mistake but unfortunately this honest mistake occasionally turns into an ongoing fraud.

When an Electronic Invoice Is Not Enough: The Double Invoicing Problem

While that old saying about taking two steps forward and then one back certainly wasn't written about electronic invoicing, it may as well have been. It probably shouldn't come as much of a surprise to those involved to learn that the transition to electronic invoicing has not gone quite as smoothly as hoped. A new problem has emerged.

The Problem

Some vendors are mailing a second paper copy of an invoice after sending the first one electronically. It should be noted that this problem is primarily with vendors who are e-mailing invoices rather than those using a third party electronic invoicing system.

In theory, the vendors are sending the second invoice to ensure at least one is received. Unfortunately, both are being received creating extra work for the accounts payable department. Even worse, in a few cases, both invoices are paid.

There is an additional concern, although to date no big cases of this have been reported. As most readers of this publication are aware, many frauds start with an honest mistake. In this case that error could be the paying of both the electronic and paper invoice.

The Solution

Make it clear to vendors when asking for electronic invoices that this means there is no need for a paper invoice as well. Beyond that, the following should help.

Step 1 Identify the vendors sending double invoices and ask them to stop. This probably won't eliminate most of your problem, but it should put a dent in it.

Step 2 Create a list of vendors who insist on sending invoices both ways and double and perhaps even triple check all payments made to them to ensure they are not being paid twice. Be especially vigilant when it comes to their paper invoices.

Step 3 If all else fails, and you can categorically identify your double senders, automatically discard paper invoices of vendors known to employ this tactic.

Step 4 This is where your good up-front controls come in to play. The three-way match should weed out these duplicates. However, that will only happen if you use rigid coding standards, extinguishing PO and receivers and your processors don't play games with the invoice number.

Step 5 Make sure invoice numbers are entered correctly. This means giving the invoice number the same careful attention given to pricing and quantity when entering invoice data. Make processors aware of this issue so they recognize the importance of entering the invoice number accurately.

This is just one example of the new problems that continue to pop up in accounts payable as we make the move from manual processing to an automated, paperless world.

Straight through processing will catch these duplicates without a problem. But for the majority who are not completely automated, manual intervention is necessary to weed out these unwanted second (and sometimes third) invoices.

CHAPTER 4
CHECKS: THE ORIGINAL (AND LEAST EFFICIENT) PAYMENT VEHICLE

Once an invoice has been approved for payment and the accounts payable department has verified that all the documents match (the proverbial three-way match), payment can be made. For most organizations, this is where checks come into play. In fact, even those organizations that make most of their payments electronically, (and those are few and far between) checks are used at least occasionally. Manually produced checks should be written only in cases of extreme emergency. In fact, it is recommended that all rush payments be made using electronic payments, i.e. ACH.

In this chapter we examine the following paper-check related issues:

- Problems caused by paper checks
- The basics of paper checks
- Ways to minimize the number of paper checks
- Techniques that will help eliminate paper checks

Headaches Caused by Paper Checks

Checks are inefficient, expensive and prone to fraud. For
starters, they are relatively expensive to produce. We're not
only talking about the obvious expenses, the cost of
purchasing check and the postage used to mail it but the
salaries of your employees who must spend their days
producing, verifying, mailing, and reconciling checks as well
as the myriad of other tasks related to the check production
cycle.

The process of producing checks is people intensive,
employees who no matter how conscientious and hard-
working they are, will occasionally introduce errors into the
process. Errors add more cost to the process as it now takes
more human intervention to fix those problems.

As discussed elsewhere in this book, check fraud continues
to be a huge problem. Incorporating the required
procedures into the mix to prevent check fraud adds more
cost to the equation.

Even the issue of mailing checks becomes complicated.
They must be taken to the mailroom right before the mail is
delivered to the post office. If taken earlier, the company is
opening itself up to the possibility that their checks will be
stolen. And, if the checks don't go to the mailroom until the
end of the day, where and how they are kept before that
becomes an issue—again introducing more elaborate
procedures (and therefore additional costs) into the check
production process.

Getting checks signed is another hassle. A discussion of who
can sign what checks and the dollar limits related to signing
authority is for another book. Just know that getting checks
signed using anything other than a signature plate as part
of the check production process adds work and expense. Yet
a good number of organizations either still require a hand
signature, or require one if the dollar amount of the check
involved is over a certain amount.

Check Stock

Care should be taken when ordering check stock. While
many organizations want to have their logo on the checks,
it is not a requirement. Some will even use their logo as a

watermark. It is important that safety features that make counterfeiting more difficult be incorporated into the check stock. Most experts consider it adequate if three safety features are incorporated into the check stock. More than three is fine, but don't go overboard.

For a long time void pantographs were considered to be a great safety device. However, they no longer work on some of the newer copy machines. Hence, Accounts Payable Now & Tomorrow strongly recommends that this not be one of the three safety features you use in your check stock.

Check Printing

When the checks are printed, they may or may not be facsimile signed depending on the corporate policy and the dollar amount of the check. After the checks are printed, they should be mailed to the intended recipients and not returned to the person requesting the check. This is a fraud control in addition to being a best practice for the accounts payable department. Checks returned to the requisitioner also have a tendency to end up as duplicate payments.

Signatures

Hand signatures are being used with much less frequency today. Typically, they are now used only on very large-dollar or emergency checks. However, with the advent of laser printer technology that can encompass a facsimile signature, even the number of hand-signed emergency checks are declining.

Double signatures are generally required on all checks over a certain dollar amount. What that dollar amount is will vary from company to company. A few companies with very good controls will allow all checks to go out the door with only one signature and that signature is generally a facsimile.

Today, at most mid-size and large companies, signatures are put on the checks during the check printing process.

Rubber Signature Stamps

The advice about rubber signature stamps is quite simple—in this day and age they are a terrible idea. Fraud using one of these stamps is laughably easy. So easy in fact that use of a rubber stamp makes a company liable for any check fraud committed using one. Not only are the stamps easy to use once thieves have gotten their hands on them, the crook can also make his own using the company's signatures once he knows the company uses them.

Voided Checks

When checks are voided, the signature portion of the check should be removed. Mark the check voided and file it away. Keep all the documentation you have regarding the reason for the void with the check. The reason for this has nothing to do with controls but everything to do with duplicate payments and unclaimed property.

Expect the unclaimed property auditor to ask to see your void file. If you don't have proper documentation the auditor may very well take the position that it is unclaimed property and the amount should be turned over to the state. It doesn't take much work to save the documentation—but without it, you could be in big trouble.

After all, the unclaimed property auditor won't show up for several years and in all likelihood no one will remember why the payment was voided in the first place.

Eliminating Paper Checks: Continued Vigilance Required

As we move ahead in the rapidly-evolving electronic payment world, paper checks will play a smaller role in the payment process. This doesn't mean we can ignore them or not employ best practices in their handling—that could mean an increase in fraud and duplicate payments. For the foreseeable future, continued vigilance over the entire paper check process is mandatory.

Five Alternatives to Paper Checks

Paper checks are a necessary evil. They are probably the most inefficient way a company can pay its bills, yet they are the way most organizations handle their invoices. What follows is a quick look at five ways any group can reduce the number of paper checks it issues followed by an explanation of three processes that will reduce the number of paper checks but are not recommended as they create more problems than they solve.

1)   **P-cards.** Start a p-card program for use on small dollar invoices. If you already have a program, look to see what else can be included in the program, further reducing the number of paper checks.

2)   **T & E reimbursements.** Where appropriate, have employees pay for something under the T&E umbrella and then submit for reimbursement along with their T&E. Of course, for this to work, proper controls must be in place to ensure the item isn't paid for twice.

3)   A credit card for accounts payable. If you don't have a p-card program consider getting one card for accounts payable and using that card to pay any invoice that can be paid using a credit card. This approach is especially successful for those organizations with lots of subscriptions. Just about every publisher takes credit cards. If your organization does have a p-card program, make sure one is issued to someone in accounts payable to pay those miscellaneous invoices that can be paid with a credit card.

4)   For those vendors who send many low-dollar invoices, consider going to a summary billing approach or paying from statements, if you can implement the proper controls to ensure no invoice will get paid, this is a real winner.

5)   Convert as many vendors to ACH as possible. We've saved the best for last. When it comes to reducing the number of paper checks being produced, this is the "killer app."

What Not to Do

1)   Refuse to pay invoices under a certain dollar amount. A few organizations have a minimum dollar amount for checks. While this may seem like a great way to reduce the number of checks written, it can backfire. While you can usually find a way to avoid issuing a check for five dollars, there may be those rare occasions when you can't. We know of one organization that stopped doing business with a vendor who took this approach.

2)   Rely on a petty cash box. Yes, paper checks are an expensive inefficient way to pay invoices, but a petty cash box is a worse way to handle your obligations. As regular readers of this publication are aware, AP Now strongly advocates for the complete elimination of petty cash boxes.

3)   Hold payments until you accumulate a certain dollar threshold and then issue a check for the total. While this may seem to make sense on one level, you could end up carrying certain balances for a very long time.

As you can see, there are a number of approaches that can be used to reduce the number of paper checks issued. Just make sure you avoid the last three. They'll create other problems much worse than paper checks. And you don't want to take one step forward and then two backwards, which is exactly what you would be doing with these three tactics.

Ways to Minimize Paper Checks

Paper checks are an expensive waste of time. Unfortunately, it isn't possible to do business without them. So at least for the foreseeable future in the United States, accounts payable is stuck with them. I emphasize the U.S. because companies in many other countries use very few, if any, paper checks.

But just because they are a necessity doesn't mean you can't take steps to reduce the number that flow through your accounts payable department. Here are six tactics you can use to reduce the number of these productivity sappers.

1. Use p-cards for all small-dollar transactions. Gradually increase the dollar threshold where cards can be used.

2. Wherever possible, instead of issuing a paper check convince the vendor to accept an electronic payment. In many cases you won't get much of an argument.

3. Insist on electronic payments via the ACH for all rush items.

4. Outsource the printing and mailing of checks to your bank.

5. If you don't have p-cards, require employees who purchase small dollar items to put in for reimbursement with their travel and entertainment expense reimbursement report rather than submitting the invoice for payment.

6. If you have many small dollar purchases from the same vendor, pay from the statement once a week or month rather than from individual invoices. This is most appropriate for office supplies, overnight mailing services, and payments for the use of temporary workers.

7. Use a ghost card for vendors where frequent small-dollar purchases are made. If you analyze your data, you just might be surprised to see how many "opportunities" you have to implement this tactic for your organization.

8. In trusted relationships, allow the vendor to tale the payment from your account via an ACH debit. This is often used to pay sales and/or use tax. Limit the accounts where the debits are permitted and reconcile them daily.

All these techniques may not work for the organizations of all readers but we believe most readers will be able to use several of them.

Please note: Use of these techniques is only recommended if you can introduce the appropriate internal controls to ensure that items will not be paid more than once using different payment vehicles.

CHAPTER 5
CORPORATE PROCUREMENT CARDS: STREAMLINING THE PAYMENT PROCESS FOR SMALL PURCHASES

Corporate procurement cards, sometimes referred to as purchase cards or p-cards, are credit cards used by employees to help them perform their jobs more efficiently. They have corporate liability. They are a great resource for reducing the number of small dollar invoices handled in the accounts payable department. Yet, despite all their obvious benefits, less than half of all organizations have p-card programs.

In this section, we take an in-depth look at:

- Crafting a p-card policy

- Common p-card problems

- Creating a purchasing card responsibility agreement (for employees)

- Additional issues and how to address them

The Corporate Procurement Card Policy

Each company should have a formal policy with regard to its p-card program. At a minimum, the p-card policy given to all affected employees, including the administrative assistants of those executives who use p-cards. It should address the following issues:

- The business case to enable employees to gain a good understanding of the importance of using the process
- A list of approved transactions
- A list of items that cannot be put on the card
- Transaction and monthly spending limits for each individual
- User procedures
- Receipt and record retention requirements for all transactions
- Procedures for the retrieval of cards from departing employees
- Procedures for lost or stolen cards
- Cardholder agreement of responsibility

The policy should be updated periodically, ideally whenever a change is made or, at a minimum, once every year. These changes should be reflected in the policy and communicated to all affected employees. It can be published on the Internet or intranet site for easy access by all employees. New employees should be given the policy as well as an overview as part of their welcome packet.

Cards and Departing Employees

As part of your exit process don't forget to include a provision for getting the card back. Additionally, as part of your exit strategies, whoever is monitoring the corporate procurement card program should be informed of all departing employees so they can cancel the cards. That way, even if the card is not retrieved the employee would not be able to use it.

The information regarding reporting the departure of employees to the group responsible for the p-card program is especially important in the case of a fired employee or one who left in a dispute. These are the employees more apt to use the card when they shouldn't after they are no longer in the company's employment. And unfortunately, these are the times when in the heat of the dispute, everyone forgets about turning off the p-card.

The information about all employee departures should be shared with the card administrator who should immediately inform the bank to cancel the card. For some reason, it is difficult for many organizations to have HR notify the appropriate personnel of employee separations. If this is the case in your organization, take one of the following steps to ensure you identify cards that should be canceled.

> 1)   Periodically get a list from HR of all active employees and compare it to the list of all cardholders. Cards held by individuals on the cardholder list but not the active employee list should be cancelled immediately.

> 2)   Periodically request a report from the card issuer showing inactive cards. Investigate all cards not being used. If the employee is no longer with the firm, immediately cancel the card. If the employee is still with the organization, question them to determine if they simply need more training on proper use of the card or if the card should be canceled, as they don't need it.

Rebates

In the past, companies that push large volume through their p-card programs have gone to their issuers and negotiated rebates based on volume. This is something that most issuers refused to talk about in the past. In fact, many contracts forbade those who receive these rebates from discussing them publicly. This is no longer the case. The issue is open for discussion and you should initiate it if the card issuer does not bring it up.

Depending on the size of the company, the rebate can be an attractive feature. Some companies, in an attempt to qualify for a larger rebate have combined their T&E cards, freight cards and p-card into what is referred to as a one-card program.

Common P-Card Problems

As with any other process related to accounts payable, there can be problems for those who don't proceed with caution. Here's a look at some of the issues that need to be investigated thoroughly before plunging headfirst into a p-card program.

Issue #1. Lack of infrastructure to support the program. It is critical that you secure senior management support, establishing a cross-functional team (e.g., purchasing, accounts payable, finance, audit, tax, etc.), and dedicating the appropriate program management personnel from the start. In addition, infrastructure includes: an effective control environment, strategies for complying with regulatory requirements (e.g., sales tax and 1099 reporting), p-card data integration with applicable systems (e.g., finance system), use of technology tools and documented policies and procedures. Many of these components are further described below. If your p-card program infrastructure is still missing something, take the necessary steps to fill the gaps. Growing a program before the infrastructure is solid will only compound the pitfalls.

Issue #2. Selecting the right administrator. Many end-user organizations, unfamiliar with what is involved with program management, do not spend enough time developing an appropriate job description and finding the right person or people for the roles. Your organization should look for a self-motivated professional with a combination of strong communication skills, analytical abilities, training experience (creating and delivering), technical abilities, knowledge of accounting principles, and past success with project leadership and management.

Issue #3. Lack of partnership with card issuer. The request for proposal (RFP) process for card issuer selection often sets the tone. One or more RFP missteps, such as rushing the process and not relaying your organization's p-card program requirements, can contribute to a business relationship that never quite becomes a partnership. However, even a well-conducted RFP can transition to a less-than-ideal situation if one or both sides (end-user and provider) fail to put forth the necessary effort for building a partnership. Discuss "roles and responsibilities" with your issuer, so that both sides are clear about each other's expectations.

Issue #4. Lack of communication to your internal organization and suppliers. Effective communication is critical for getting people to embrace the process changes associated with p-card program implementation. Your organization should convey the p-card business case, tailoring the message to fit each audience. Suppliers, for example, need to be educated on how p-card acceptance will help them. Furthermore, communicate your p-card -related requirements to suppliers, addressing items such as the order process, documentation, and card/account data security.

Issue #5. Ineffective training. A mandated training program is essential and commonplace. However, if employees are not learning what they are supposed to, it can be equated with no training at all. There are, of course, a variety of possible training methods and styles. Regardless of method, your organization should have ways to identify the effectiveness of the training; for example, survey program participants about their training experience to gauge their satisfaction and track cardholders' compliance with program policies and procedures to evaluate their comprehension.

Issue #6. Incomplete documentation of policies and procedures. First and foremost, policies and procedures must be documented. Then, editing for brevity and clarity can only improve the outcome. P-card policies and procedures should align with program goals, not conflict with other organizational policies and procedures and must be updated as the program changes and grows. How frequently does your organization review and revise its policies and procedures?

Issue #7. Over or under controlling the program. The ultimate challenge is striking the right balance of controls, with effectiveness being more important than the sheer number of controls. Auditing every transaction for every cardholder every period reduces the process savings inherent to p-cards. A better long-term approach is for an organization to review the cost versus benefit and consider its level of risk tolerance. Does your organization want to spend, for example, $200 to find a $20 issue? If an organization with a 100% audit process finds few—or even no—serious infractions, it may want to consider something other than a "100% approach"; for example, adjusting its process to suit its appetite for risk, whether this means auditing 10%, 20% or other percentage of transactions.

Issue #8. Complicated or inefficient processes. For utmost efficiency, do not simply add p-card payment to the end of a current, inefficient procure-to-pay process; this provides little benefit to your organization and its suppliers. The key is to eliminate the inefficiencies, re-engineering the "traditional process," which is often paper-based, involving a requisition, purchase order and check payment. If p-cards are difficult to use, involving, for example, more steps, documentation and restrictions/rules than other procure-to-pay processes, employees will be disgruntled and the program will stall. Your organization should pursue electronic reporting, data integration between systems, online statement delivery, electronic review and approvals and, whenever appropriate, automatic transaction reconciliation.

Issue #9. Ineffective card distribution. Cards may be in the wrong hands, under-distributed, and/or over-distributed. First, determine which employees tend to initiate purchases or requisitions, as they are prime targets for the cardholder role.

Issuing a card to just one employee per department may represent under-distribution, as that one employee may have nothing to do with some of the purchasing activity within his or her area. Similarly, over-distribution is also a potential problem, usually resulting in a high number of inactive cards.

Create Your Own Purchasing Cardholder Responsibility Agreement

With the right to use a corporate procurement card comes certain responsibilities. And obviously it's important that every cardholder understands just what those responsibilities are. They should be spelled out as part of the p-card policy and procedures manual (which can be a section of the accounts payable policy and procedures manual).

Ideally, these are printed and given to the cardholder along with the card. He or she should be asked to sign a letter saying they understand what their responsibilities are and that if they use the card inappropriately their employment can be terminated.

Here is a list of typical cardholder responsibilities you can use to create your own cardholder responsibility agreement. Cardholders who accept a p-card agree to:

- Sign the signature panel on the card immediately upon receipt of the card.

- Be responsible for using the card in accordance with the organization's policies and procedures and any applicable procurement regulations.

- Retain receipts, sales slips, and other purchase documentation as spelled out in the organization's p-card policy.

- Maintain appropriate card security to prevent unauthorized charges against the account.

- Obtain a receipt at the point of purchase and verify it for accuracy immediately.

- Reconcile receipts and other purchase documentation to the cardholder statement.

- Call the p-card administrator immediately to:

1. Report lost or stolen cards.

2. Notify the p-card administrator of any billing discrepancies posted on the cardholder statement that cannot be resolved with the merchant.

3. Notify the p-card administrator of and name, telephone, address or other changes that could affect the account.

- Forward the reconciled statement, purchase documentation, and all associated receipts/charge slips to the designated approver for review.
- Deny use of this card to any member of their staff or supervisor.
- Not use the card for personal expenditures.

How P-cards Got A Bad Reputation: Fixing the Problem

When used properly, p-cards can make the accounts payable process go a lot smoother. Their value with small dollar purchases just skyrocketed given that the card issuer will now have responsibility for 1099 reporting instead of the purchaser. Yet, many organizations still don't use them.

We've identified eight common problems and offer easy solutions to each of them. You will note that we take a pretty stern view on proper p-card policies and procedures.

The Problem: The cardholder uses the card for personal use.

The Solution: The organization's policy should expressly forbid this. The cardholder should sign a letter when receiving the card indicating he or she understands if they misuse the card they can be terminated. One time violations might be allowed although the employee should be spoken to about it. If the card is used a second time, the employee should be terminated. In all likelihood only one or two employees will be terminated as the rest of the company will realize the policy is being enforced.

The Problem: Cardholders make unauthorized purchases on the card.

The Solution: The policy should be quite detailed indicating what is permitted and what is not. One time violations might be allowed although the employee should be spoken to about it. If the card is used a second time, the employee should be terminated.

The Problem: Cardholders don't keep their card information private.

The Solution: The policy should prohibit the sharing of cards or card information. If it comes to the attention of the card staff or the manager the employee should be spoken to about it. If information has been shared, the card should be canceled and a new one issued. If information is shared a second time, the employee should lose his or her card privileges. If this results in an inability to perform their job, termination may be the only choice.

The Problem: Cardholders don't maintain the appropriate records and receipts.

The Solution: For starters, the policy should spell out exactly what each cardholder is expected to do regarding their p-card activity. Failure to follow the rules should be treated as any other serious job-related abuse and the consequences should be the same.

The Problem: Cardholders verify or approve their own transactions.

The Solution: Clearly this is a problem. When a card is issued, the approver is also designated. His or her responsibilities are spelled out in the policy. If the approver defaults this responsibility back to the purchaser, the approver should be spoken to about it. This is a serious dereliction of duties. If the practice continues, termination of the negligent approver should be considered.

The Problem: Cardholder has purchases shipped to their home rather than the office.

The Solution: While no malice may be intended this is a bad practice to allow as it opens the door to fraud. The policy should require all purchases to go through the normal mail delivery and verification. Violations of this practice should be taken seriously as it could indicate an employee testing the waters for a future fraud. Again, this should be a two strikes and you're out policy violation.

The Problem: Cardholders split a transaction to make a purchase that is above their maximum dollar limits on the card.

The Solution: First the policy should clearly prohibit this practice. Violations should be considered on a case-by-case basis. If the infringement is serious enough, i.e. the cardholder was trying to avoid getting approval for something that would not be approved otherwise the cardholder should be terminated on the first infraction. If it appears to be an honest mistake, let the employee off with a warning and a clear explanation that the next time will mean the loss of the job.

The Problem: Cards from terminated employees are not canceled.

The Solution: The risks in this case are obvious and the recourse the company has is limited. Hence it is critical that this issue be handled correctly. Any time an employee terminates his or her employment, the card should be cancelled. This is whether the employee chose to leave or the company asked the employee to leave. HR should notify the card administrator and the bank should be contacted to cancel the card. Ideally, the card should be returned but this often doesn't happen. The overriding issue is to get the information to the bank quickly so a disgruntled employee will not have the chance to use the card for personal purchases. This is the biggest issue missed by most companies and the one they have complete control over.

The Problem: Cardholders neglect to inform the company when their card is lost or stolen. Sometimes this is because they do not keep it in a secure location and are not aware the card has been taken.

The Solution: The policy should lay out the cardholder's responsibilities for the safekeeping of the card given to them. They should also be given instructions on what to do if the card is lost or stolen. It is probably not a bad idea to send these instructions to all cardholders once a year.

By now you've probably noticed that eliminating bad habits with regard to p-cards starts with your written policy. It should be as detailed as possible so no one can point a finger to an issue not addressed. Not only should it spell out what is expected and where the card can and cannot be used, it should make it patently clear what the consequences are for policy violations. The accompanying table shows a list of practices you might want to prohibit in your policy. If you've not updated the policy in a year or two (or longer) perhaps it's time for a review.

We hear talk of policies of zero tolerance when it comes to fraud and T&E abuse. P-cards should be included in that discussion. They are a wonderful tool for any organization. Don't let a few poor practices stand in the way of your organization from having a top notch p-card program.

Bad P-card Practices the Policy Should Ban

Certain practices, as they relate to corporate procurement cards tend to weaken controls. Some of the practices that should be prohibited include:

- The sharing of cards or card information between employees as this makes it difficult, if not impossible, to identify a culprit in case of misuse of the card

- The delivery of goods to the home instead of the office, although with an increasing number of employees working from home either all or part of the time, this restriction could present some challenges

- The purchaser and approver being the same person as this results in a complete lack of segregation of duties

• Split transactions as they are often used to circumvent controls and spending authorization limits

• Personal use of the card as this can blur the lines between appropriate and inappropriate use

CHAPTER 6
ELECTRONIC PAYMENTS: THE MOST
EFFICIENT PAYMENT PROCESS

We talk a lot about ACH payments but realize that not everyone understands the nuances of ACH. So, we've included some basic questions and answers designed to provide you with the fundamental knowledge needed to understand how the ACH operates. It is based on material provided by the National Automated Clearing House Association (NACHA). Given the growth of corporate use of ACH to pay its invoices, it is critical that all accounts payable professionals understand how this network operates.

In this chapter we review critical information related to electronic payments including:

- Basic definitions
- Frequently asked questions about ACH
- How to start a program
- Issues to consider when expanding a program
- Pitfalls to avoid

ACH Primer: Credits, Debits

With the sudden onslaught of interest in ACH from both businesses and unfortunately crooks, a review of the basics of how ACH works is in order. For without a thorough understanding of how these payment vehicles work, it is difficult for an organization to protect itself. We cannot underestimate the importance of understanding this payment tool as both users and non-users are at risk for various types of fraud if they do not take the appropriate steps. And then of course, there is the added benefit of ACH payments being a more efficient way to address invoices.

The Basics: ACH Credits

An ACH credit is a payer-initiated transaction. The payer instructs its financial institution to electronically transmit the payment through the ACH/Federal Reserve network to the payee's bank account. Typically the funds are available the day after the transaction takes place. This eliminates all delays associated with mail and processing float.

The most common examples of this are direct deposit of payroll, where the employer is the payer and the employee the payee. One of the biggest users of this type of payment vehicle is the Federal government when it direct deposits Social Security payments. In this case the recipients are the payees receiving benefits. Companies offering direct deposit of payroll have long taken advantage of ACH credits.

In recent years, businesses of all sorts have started making payments using the ACH instead of paper checks or in some cases, wire transfers. Because of the connection to direct deposit, this has led some to refer to this type of payment as a 'direct payment.'

The Basics: ACH Debits

An ACH debit is a payee-initiated transaction. The payee instructs the payer's financial institution to electronically transmit the payment through the ACH/Federal Reserve network to the payee's bank account. Typically the funds are available the day after the transaction takes place. These transactions are initiated using your bank transit and routing number and your bank account number. It is implied that you have given your consent but there is no formal verification process by the bank to ensure you have given your approval. There are new bank products just emerging that provide some protection against unauthorized debits.

The most common examples of the use of ACH debits is in the financial services sector. Some financial institutions granting mortgages will, with the payer's permission, debit the payer's bank account for the agreed amount on an agreed upon date each month. Sometimes there is a slight reduction in the mortgage rate in exchange for this arrangement. The insurance industry has also used this approach with some of its products.

This payment vehicle has also migrated to the business community. Some states collect their sales and use tax using this approach. A few organizations make intercompany transfers this way. In a couple of rare instances ACH debits are negotiated as part of the terms and conditions in a sales agreement. While we never expect to see ACH debits play a prominent part in the payment world, they are a vehicle that will play a continuing role. It is critical that every professional involved with payments understand them because they are used by fraudsters in growing numbers.

ACH credits and debits are the payment vehicle of the future. It is imperative that we all understand how they work and what can go wrong, if they are not handled correctly. As noted above, banks are not currently verifying if ACH debits are authorized, unless certain fraud prevention products are purchased from them. And occasionally, crooks are finding ways to circumvent these controls either by developing a workaround or simply devising a new fraud. Thus it is imperative that everyone not only know how the payment vehicles work, they understand frauds currently being perpetrated and how to prevent those frauds. This is an area that is constantly changing.

FAQs about ACH

Besides understanding the rudimentary underpinnings of the two basic types of payments, there's more information you need to understand when it comes to payments made via the ACH. The following questions and answers will help in that regard.

> • **What is the Automated Clearing House Network?** The Automated Clearing House (ACH) Network is the backbone for the electronic movement of money and payment-related data. It provides a safe, secure, electronic network for direct consumer, business, and government payments, and annually facilitates billions of Direct Deposit via ACH and Direct Payment via ACH transactions. The Network, which is

used by all types of financial institutions, is governed by the fair and equitable NACHA Operating Rules, which guide risk management and create payment certainty for all participants.

- **How does it work?** The ACH Network is a batch processing system in which financial institutions accumulate ACH transactions throughout the day for later batch processing. Instead of using paper to carry necessary transaction information, such as with checks, ACH Network transactions are transmitted electronically, allowing for faster processing times and cost savings.

- **What types of payments does it handle?** The ACH Network processes two types of transactions: Direct Deposits via ACH and Direct Payments via ACH.

- **What is Direct Deposit?** Direct Deposit via ACH is the deposit of funds for payroll, employee expense reimbursement, government benefits, tax and other refunds, and annuities and interest payments. It includes any ACH credit payment from a business or government to a consumer.

- **What is Direct Payment?** Direct Payment via ACH is the use of funds to make a payment. Individuals or organizations can make a Direct Payment via ACH as either an ACH credit or debit.

- **How do Direct Payment credit transactions work?** A Direct Payment processed as an ACH credit pushes funds into an account. An example of this is when a consumer initiates a payment through his/her bank or credit union to pay a bill.

- **How do Direct Payment debit transactions work?** A Direct Payment processed as an ACH debit pulls funds from an account. An example of this is when a consumer establishes a recurring monthly payment for a mortgage or utility bill, and his/her account is debited automatically. ACH credit and ACH debit transactions process quickly. Settlement, or the transfer of funds from one financial institution to another to complete the transaction, generally takes only one business days.

- **What is the settlement time for Direct Payments?** Specifically, the NACHA Operating Rules require that ACH credits settle in one to two business days and ACH debits settle on the next business day.

Starting an ACH Payment Program

Without a doubt, at some point in the next decade, every organization will make at least part if not all of their payments electronically. Many have already started to do so. Others are considering programs now—or will be in the near future when an 800-pound-gorilla supplier insists on electronic payments. If you haven't yet started an electronic program, what follows is a look at some of the issues you should consider before launching one. Readers should note that they will sometimes hear ACH payments referred to as direct payments, a play on direct deposit of payroll.

Start with the Bank

The first place you need to go if you want to pay using ACH is to the bank where your checking account is. The bank officer assigned to your account should be able to put you in touch with the right personnel in the bank. He or she will help you get set up and offer you some advice on converting vendors. Don't contact any vendor until you are comfortable with the process the bank suggests. You may have to make certain adjustments to your processes or accounting system and in all likelihood this will require technical support.

Depending on who has the relationship with the bank, it may be necessary to get treasury or accounting involved. Only when you have the banking, accounting, and IT concerns under control should you consider your first electronic payment.

Crawling before You Walk

A good way to get started, says a controller we spoke with, is to begin paying employee expense reimbursements by ACH. This will save money for the company (the cost of printing checks) and time for the employees (no need to make a trip to the bank to deposit reimbursement checks). Also, it will give the accounts payable department an opportunity to get used to the process. It should be an easy set up since payroll should have the direct deposit info on file so there is an opportunity to have a few "good wins" in the transition.

Once everyone is comfortable with the process, she advises, begin contacting your vendors and asking if it is possible to make payments electronically. This step should be taken with some care. Some who have contacted all their vendors at one time have learned the hard way— when the positive response was much higher than they anticipated—that they couldn't accommodate everyone at once.

The controller explains this can happen because most companies are happy to accept electronic payments, as it reduces their processing costs (no taking checks to the bank) and the funds received are verified (no bounced checks). ACH payments are typically free to receive, so they also avoid bank and in-house processing costs and eliminate the "float".

The Cash Flow Impact

Our readers, warns the controller, should also consider that transitioning to ACH payments will have an impact on cash flow (no float) as the money will be withdrawn from their account typically within two days of initiating the transfer. Therefore, it's important that those doing cash flow forecasting be included in the ACH planning. More than one accounts payable manager has ended up with egg on his or her face after implementing what they thought was a great program only to have cash flow fall short of what was planned and management less than pleased with the outcome.

There is a relatively simple solution to this problem, although it will take some planning and management support. Many organizations renegotiate their payment terms to take an extra two or three days to make the transaction float neutral.

Auditors really like ACH payments, points out the controller, since there are no checks sitting around on someone's desk waiting to be mailed. She also notes that controllers are also happy due to fewer outstanding items on the bank reconciliation at the end of the month. Given the rough economic times many organizations currently face, do not down play the importance of cash flow.

Getting Vendor Information

An accounting manager we spoke with explained how he verifies bank information. "We require a copy of a cancelled check, a copy of a deposit ticket or ACH instructions on company letterhead maybe with an office signature to verify information," he says.

This step is taken to insure that no one inserts their own bank information. Some organizations will only take the voided check or deposit ticket. The opportunity for fraud is high here, although to be honest there have only been a limited number of reports of this type of fraud.

Other Considerations

There are other issues to take into consideration when starting a program. They include:

> ▪ Be careful who you invite. If you have any thoughts of paying a particular vendor with a credit card in the future, do not invite them to participate in your program. It will be difficult to convert them from ACH to p-card, so better to avoid the issue completely.

> ▪ Depending on the accounting system in use, it may still be possible to do a separate "check run" in AP for electronic payments so that the record-keeping is easier. If the accounting system in use does not allow for this, then the reader should consider how these records will be kept.

> ▪ Consider creating a FAQ brochure for vendors answering the most common questions. This preemptive approach can help overcome objections before they occur.

> ▪ Once you have contacted all vendors, look for other ways to get vendors into your ACH program. One of the easiest is to insist that all rush payments will be made by ACH, not paper check. In many cases once they receive one payment electronically, they'll never want to go back to paper.

Whether or not you have a program now, electronic payments will play a big part in the payment world of the future.

Critical Issues to Evaluate when Considering a Move/or an Expansion of an ACH

It seems like everywhere you turn in the accounts payable world, the elimination of paper checks is a best practice recommendation. And, with good reason; checks are costly and create lots of problems. Electronic payments are definitely cheaper and create far fewer problems. However, rushing ahead without taking into account the full ramification of a move to electronic payments is not a smart course of action. You need to understand what you are getting into, where the benefits are as well what pitfalls you might encounter. Once you understand that, you can craft a plan that will allow you to enter the electronic payment arena or expand you current program wisely.

The Hidden Benefits

Here are a few considerations to take into account when making the move to an electronic payment platform. We'll start by looking at the issues that will add value to your operations.

> • *Unclaimed property.* Since there are no un-cashed checks, there are no escheat issues related to payments made this way. If a payment bounces, it will come back in a day or two and most firms track down the rightful owner at that point.

> • *Bank account reconciliations.* Since there should be no outstanding items, bank account reconciliations should be easier for these items. What's more, many organizations balance these accounts daily so in effect the bank recs are done before you start.

Operational Issues

The following issues need to be addressed and perhaps your current practices adjusted before you plunge into the electronic payment waters in a meaningful way.

> ▪ *Float.* Since the payment you initiate today will hit the payee's bank tomorrow, the mail and processing float are squeezed out of the equation. Some who find this objectionable, despite all the other savings, have renegotiated payment terms with their suppliers to make the transactions float neutral. For the most part, they split the float period. Since most people believe that mail and processing float is about five days, adding two or three days to the payment terms is generally considered acceptable. However, this should be discussed with suppliers rather than taken arbitrarily. If the float issue is not

fully explored and the organization rushes ahead without fully analyzing it, they may get an ugly cash flow surprise when the payments all hit on one day instead of being spread out over a week or so.

▪ *Fraud issues.* While a move to electronic payments will impact check fraud problems, it will not completely eliminate all other payment fraud concerns. It would be naive to think that other fraud considerations would disappear. Steps you can and should take to guard against ACH fraud. Note that some of these steps should be taken whether your organization makes electronic payments or not. But do not fall into the trap of thinking you can let up your guard with regards to check fraud. You can't. You must be as vigilant as ever with regards to potential check fraud.

▪ *Strong up-front controls.* Since there is no signature on the payment, strong up-front controls are crucial as there is no signer "available" to catch errors. While it is true that signers shouldn't be catching mistakes, in reality they often do. So, if your signers regularly catch mistakes on checks, you might want to tighten your up-front controls before rushing full throttle into the electronic payment arena.

▪ *Vendors.* There are vendor issues related to cash application. While one would think that vendors would be clamoring to be paid electronically, this has not turned out to be the case. Apparently some systems have trouble applying cash received electronically. Thus, some of your vendors may be reluctant to accept payments electronically despite the obvious benefits. Devise ways such as sending a separate email or creating a vendor website to ensure that your suppliers' AR staffs can get the information they need to apply cash.

▪ *Staff reluctance to change.* As with any new initiative, expect to find some staff dragging their feet and complaining about the change. It goes with the territory. Explain the benefits to them.

▪ *Headcount.* The reality is once your program is up and running, you'll need fewer people to process checks, if you've managed to convert a significant portion of your vendors to the process. Eventually, you will need fewer people in this area. The important thing to note is the "eventually." Converting vendors actually takes time so it is recommended that your conversion efforts go out to only a portion of your vendor base. Once you've processed every vendor who signs up, start with another portion. When you've gotten the majority of your suppliers on board you may have an extra staffer or two. They can be assigned to more value added work.

Paying through the ACH rather than paper checks makes for a more efficient accounts payable process. Organizations everywhere are making the switch. Some are doing it a little at a time while others are attempting to get large portions of their supplier base converted as quickly as possible. Whichever approach you choose, do it wisely taking all the factors discussed above into account.

It's only a matter of time before we're making the lion's share of our payments this way. The federal government is leading the way in the US - again. It has announced that all benefit payments after March 1, 2013 will be made electronically. Paper checks will not be cut. What about your organization? How long will it take to catch up with the feds when it comes to making electronic payments?

Avoid These ACH 'Gotchas' for ACH Success

Speeding up cash disbursements isn't an approach most organizations willingly adopt. It's even worse when the move is unexpected—something that somehow never happens when the organization is flush with cash. (It always seems to occur when cash is tight.) Yet, that is exactly what can happen when an organization moves from checks to ACH if they don't plan ahead and make the appropriate changes in payment terms. Whenever an organization makes a change in procedures, it is crucial that thought be given to all the ramifications; the move to ACH is no exception. We recently asked readers of our ezine who've made the move to ACH what issues others should expect so they can avoid fallout.

Extinguishing POs and Receivers

One of the first issues that come to mind is a surprising metric. While most checks payments are made through accounts payable, the same cannot be said for ACH payments. In a good number of organizations ACH payments are also initiated in other departments.

A very real concern is that the other departments might not extinguish the POs and open receivers opening the organization to another potential avenue for duplicate payments. We believe if others are to make ACH payments, it's crucial that adequate training be provided to those individuals. Open POs and receivers can result in duplicate payments should a second invoice be presented.

Additionally, state auditors could construe the open receiver as unclaimed property. And, if you think this is something I'm making up, let me warn you that a few organizations are fighting with state auditors over this very issue right now. Should the auditors win, they will be looking at every organization's open receivers when they come for an audit.

Open receivers can cause a misstatement of your financial records if those receivers are used for accrual purposes. If there are enough of them, the misstatement could be material. This is something no one wants hanging over them.

Obviously these issues are avoided if the organization insists that ACH payments must flow through the AP system.

Setup Time Involved

"Our ERP software for the pay cycle was setup to create ACH files from these invoices but the output was nothing like what was required from the bank," reports an AP manager who requests anonymity. She notes that her staff spent endless hours completing the process to automate ACH payments. The company cut ACH payments for over 30 companies and all activity is now output to a file that is uploaded to its bank once a day. While the time savings once the process was in place is impressive, underestimating the time and effort needed to get the ACH process up and running can come back to haunt you.

This company was not home free once they had the process working, however. When they merged with another organization, they had to integrate their ACH payments with their new partners'. In this case the treasury department was involved and coordination became an issue.

Cash Flow Implications

Changing to ACH has a direct and immediate effect on cash flow. "ACHs clear the next day while your checks require mail time and deposit time at the bank, which could leave the funds in your account anywhere from three to ten days," points out an accounts payable/receivable manager.

One way to compensate for the immediate disbursal of funds, she says, would be to extend your payments to vendors a few days longer. So if you would normally cut a check on, say, May 16th wait until the 22nd to make the ACH payment. In fact, many organizations anticipate the cash flow impact and renegotiate terms with their vendors at the time they move to ACH. Those who ignore this issue will have a rude awakening the first time the ACH payments hit.

Depending on how tight the cash flow is in your organization, this could be the worst problem of all and the one with the highest visibility. If the company runs out of cash and the cause of the liquidity crisis is identified as the move to ACH without an accompanying renegotiating of payment terms, the results will not be pretty. This is *not* how any employee wants to come to the attention of upper management.

The Cash App Issue

The remittance advice can be problematic since there is no check stub for the vendor to see what invoices are being paid. The accounts payable/receivable manager mentioned earlier prints off remittance advices and e-mails them to the vendors. She notes she could mail it but the payment would arrive before the remittance advice. She also points out that when vendors don't know how to apply payments, they call. And that adds more work to the accounts payable department partially offsetting the productivity gains from going electronic.

Finally, if the remittance advice is mailed, the postage cost savings goes away. Use of the ACH for payment processes can result in significant savings for the organization. However, like any new process, if the full ramifications are not explored its implementation can make the process worse rather than better. By addressing the issues discussed above, you will be well on your way to avoiding an ACH implementation debacle.

CHAPTER 7
OPERATIONAL ISSUES:
INVOICE HANDLING AND PROCESSING

Invoice handling is the primary reason for the existence of any accounts payable department. In general, they are also the document that creates the most headaches for any accounts payable group. In this section we look at the following invoice problems:

- Duplicate invoices
- Invoices without identifiers as to who placed the order
- Discrepant invoices
- All other invoice challenges

Since automation plays such a key role in running a more efficient accounts payable function, we also highlight how it can help with certain invoice problems.

Weeding out Duplicate Invoices

It would be nice if vendors would send one invoice and then wait for their payment. However, that doesn't always happen. When the payment isn't received by the due date, most vendors will send a second invoice. These are often not marked as a duplicate invoice or a copy of an invoice. It then falls to the accounts payable department to identify these unwanted seconds.

The Problem Gets Worse

Duplicate invoices have always been a problem. In the past they were typically sent only in the case of a late payment. That is now changing. Some vendors now send two invoices and this is creating massive headaches for the accounts payable staff who receive them.

There is an emerging problem of vendors emailing (or faxing) invoices and then for good measure because they want to make sure the invoice arrives, also mailing it as well. Whether the rationale for submitting the second invoice is devious or honest is irrelevant. It still means more work for accounts payable. That's why you need top-notch practices to identify these problematic second invoices.

The Game Plan

To deal with this issue, employing the following tactics will help identify and eliminate the duplicate invoices:

1. Identify those vendors sending by postal mail and e-mail and ask them to stop sending one of the ways. Occasionally, just asking vendors to stop sending multiple invoices solves the problem. However, many don't for a variety of reasons. Hence, it is critical to know who's doing this and utilize extra checking routines on these vendors.

2. Centralize the receipt of invoices. This ensures accounts payable knows of all invoices as early in the cycle as possible. It also makes it less likely that a duplicate will slip through.

3. Insist that the accounts payable staff processing invoices uses standardized routines and rigid coding standards. This means that everyone who processes invoices uses exactly the same procedures. It also means setting up a coding standard for everyone to use when entering data so all data is entered the same, regardless of who enters the information. This step is critical. If you don't employ this step it is likely that duplicates will slip through.

4. Strong internal controls from the moment the invoice arrives in your office until the payment leaves are also an important component in any approach to eliminate duplicate invoices. This should apply not only to invoices sent through the postal mail, but also electronic invoices, as well.

5. Create an Always-Check-Thoroughly (ACT) list of vendors who routinely submit duplicate invoices. This will include not only those who submit through multiple channels but also those who are likely to send duplicates for other reasons.

6. Don't overlook the importance of staff training. When employees are first hired they should be trained by the most knowledgeable person available for the task. Periodically review their work to determine if additional training might be warranted. And, anytime a new process or procedure is introduced make sure everyone who might need it is given a thorough explanation of how the new process will work. Don't assume they will all figure it out. Also, update your policy and procedures manual with the new procedures so any employee who has questions can check on his or her own.

7. Don't overlook the benefits afforded by technology. With invoice automation, the task of identifying duplicates is a simple. Computers do an excellent job identifying duplicate invoices.

When all is said and done, sometimes despite the very best efforts of the accounts payable staff, a few duplicates do slip through and get paid. Unfortunately, rarely are those second payments returned by the vendors who received them unless some nudged by the vendor or its representatives. That's why a payment audit is highly recommended as a last step to identify those cases where an extra payment was made. Payment audits should be part of every best-practice accounts payable function.

To ensure that the payment auditors find as little as possible, implement as many of the steps described above as you can.

Invoices without Identifiers:
No Name, No Purchase Order Number

Invoices that arrive in the mail addressed to no one at the company create big headaches for accounts payable—when they finally get there! They typically wend their way through the company eventually ending up in accounts payable. And that's when and where the fun begins. The already overworked staff in accounts payable then has to try and figure out who ordered the goods so they can get the invoice approved for payment. And to make matters worse, if you think most of these wayward children have PO numbers on them, you are mistaken. Of course, these are suppliers who call looking for payment even before the invoice finally arrives in accounts payable.

A reader wrote in to *Accounts Payable Now & Tomorrow* to ask for our help with this problem. When we ran this story in our e-zine, *e-News from the AP Front*, the response was overwhelming: the invoices should be sent back to the supplier requesting more information. Several of our readers elaborated on a variety of practices that can be implemented by all companies wishing to employ best invoice handling practices. Here are some samples.

Put the Monkey Back on the Suppliers Back

"Invoices not mailed to the attention of the accounts payable department alone are a problem, but not having a purchase order only adds fuel to the problem. The company I work for agrees with me that such invoices be returned to the vendor," writes one professional. She attaches a letter noting it needs a purchase order to be processed.

This puts the problem back on the vendor, who should have not taken an order without a purchase order. The vendor then contacts the individual in the writer's organization who placed the order—who should have created a purchase order for the vendor in the first place. "This is just our way of putting the problem back into the hands of the people who started the whole problem," she notes. This accounts payable professional has found that this type of problem has declined since the company started returning invoices.

A Strong Mail Policy

"First of all, anything that appears to be an invoice should go directly to accounts payable," points out another writer. Whether a company has a full-fledged mailroom or the receptionist sorts the mail, invoices should be handled that way in this SOX world. Any mail distribution should have a system for every kind of mail.

Systems Help

Another reader's tip: have your ERP system print a "No PO" letter every week to send suppliers, listing the invoice(s) in question. The letter should state that POs are required or at the very least provide the full name of the employee who ordered the goods or service. Keep the original invoice and enter it with no account distribution so it automatically goes on hold. This AP pro uses Oracle and says this may be an Oracle perk but other systems can probably handle it as well.

Education

"Most suppliers know they need a PO or at least the name of the person who ordered the product," writes a subscriber. "The trick is to educate not only the supplier, but the organization's employees as well." Thus, some firms are quite insistent on after the fact POs. They figure, probably correctly, that if the employees know they are going to have to issue a PO eventually, they will do it in the beginning instead of trying to take a short cut and not bother with it.

"Having been around the block several times (35 years)," writes another reader, "the willingness to accept invoices without POs or even the name of the purchaser indicates that poor internal controls are acceptable and a way of life at this company." In today's age there is no excuse for this practice." At his organization there is a strict policy that everything must be _approved_ through the use of electronic requisitions. The size of the company does not matter.

There are many canned software packages, the writer points out, that will allow this to be done over personal computers on a WAN (at minimal cost) as well as the more sophisticated packages for mainframes. He also notes the old excuse that it takes too long to enter a requisition is complete bunk. If done right this can be accomplished with a setup where a requisition can be approved in minutes authorizing the creation of a purchase order and issuing it.

The folks who usually complain about the time it takes to prepare an electronic requisition are the same ones who don't do the paper requisitions. This veteran agrees with *Accounts Payable Now & Tomorrow* and would quickly junk any no-return of invoices policy and mandate all purchases be supported by purchase orders with the explicit direction given on the header of the purchase order that all invoices are to be mailed to "Accounts Payable." "Better yet, he concludes, provide an e-mail for supplier to send invoices in pdf format." We couldn't agree more.

A Plan to Ensure Discrepant Invoices Don't Create a Financial Debacle for Your Company

It's great when the three-way match works and the invoice can be processed and paid without further intervention. Unfortunately, that does not always happen. The frequency of mismatches will depend on many issues, including but not limited to: the quality of your purchase orders, your industry, damages during shipment, the accuracy of the invoices etc.

If discrepancies between invoices, purchasing documents and receivers are not resolved quickly, the due date will come and go without a payment. While some may be thinking "so what's the problem, we held onto our money for a little longer" savvy professionals know that late payments can lead to additional work and an occasional duplicate payment. Once an invoice goes past due, the odds are high that a second— and sometimes a third—invoice will be sent by the vendor in an attempt to get paid. These require extra work to weed them out, even if they are not paid. What's more, late payments lead to frayed vendor relationships.

The Game Plan

To ensure your discrepant invoices don't end up eating into your organization's profitability, take the following actions.

- **Step 1:** Establish a routine for tracking discrepant invoices. If this can be pulled from your accounting system, take that route. If not, the manager can track this information in an Excel spreadsheet.

- **Step 2**: Schedule regular follow ups on all discrepant invoices. Whoever is responsible for resolving the problems (and it is usually the invoice processors), should be instructed to follow-up on a regular basis. This might be every 48 hours or maybe once a week. This will depend on, among other issues, your industry, how many discrepant invoices a processor typically has and corporate culture.

- **Step 3**: Pull regular reports for review. This data is only worthwhile if it is used aggressively to eliminate the discrepant invoice problem. See the discussion below regarding Data to make sure you have included all the relevant information needed to get the most out of this exercise.

- **Step 4:** Analyze the data from the regular reports to identify problematic processors, vendors and purchasers. Additionally, identify weaknesses in your processes that might be responsible for the problems and see what can be done to tighten these procedures.

- **Step 5:** Age your discrepant invoices and publish a report of the oldest unresolved invoice problems, along with the processor responsible for the invoice. This can be kept within the department. Typically, it is a list no one wants to be on the top of and it can help motivate processors to work those really ugly problems.

Data to Include

In order for anyone to be able to use this information effectively, it is important that certain pieces of information be included. For starters, this would include:

- Vendor
- Invoice number
- Invoice data
- Processor
- Purchaser

Once the problem is resolved, update the report to show what the problem was and how it was resolved. These pieces of information are critical if you are to identify process changes that need to be made to avoid problems in the future.

By looking to see if a large number of discrepant invoices are coming from one vendor, purchaser or processor you will be in the best position to identify situations where additional training might be required.

For this process to work effectively, it is critical that processors enter invoice data as soon as they receive invoices. Don't let them keep problematic invoices on their desk in a folder. This makes it difficult to complete an accurate analysis of discrepant invoices.

Finally, it should be every accounts payable department's goal to resolve discrepant invoice problems before due date so the invoice can be paid on time. With this approach, the Discrepant Invoice Aging report should be quite short.

Other Invoice Challenges in a Paper World

No matter how automated an organization, virtually all still are plagued by paper invoices. Of course, some have done a fabulous job getting rid of a large number of them, but many others still face the unenviable task of processing mountains of paper. In this article we take a look at eight invoice challenges in a paper world, discuss some solutions as well as offer a brief commentary on if and how automation might help.

Challenge: Errors in Manual Data Entry

Tips in a Paper World: Without a doubt, human keying errors create problems for just about any organization entering data manually. Running batch totals is one way to verify that at a minimum, payment amounts have been entered correctly. Some organizations have found that allowing processors to listen to music (with headsets on so others are not disturbed) helps reduce errors also. Finally, a coding standard will help eliminate those errors created when processors are allowed to create their own abbreviations and shortcuts.

How Automation Helps: By eliminating the data entry function, automation eliminates those keying errors made by processors.

Challenge: Lack of Consistency when Data Is Entered Manually

Tips in a Paper World: This is one of the easiest problems to create a solution for. A rigid coding standard along with rigid procedures will eliminate the problem. With every processor handling invoices exactly the same way, errors associated with different handling procedures are eliminated. It is not enough to create the ideal process and coding standard, managers need to periodically check to make sure all processors are sticking to the standards and not introducing their own work arounds.

How Automation Helps: Processors handling invoices differently is not a problem in a completely automated invoice processing environment.

Challenge: Receipt of Invoices

Tips in a Paper World: In a paper world, invoices are often sent to a variety of places. Some come to accounts payable, some are addressed to no one and are passed from person to person until someone realizes they belong in accounts payable and others are sent to the original purchaser. When invoices don't come directly to accounts payable, additional work is created when vendors call looking for payments on invoices still with approvers. In an ideal paper world (Is that an oxymoron?) invoices are sent to one centralized location for further distribution. This way they can be logged and tracked.

With organizations everywhere looking to cut costs, a number of vendors are refusing to mail invoices. They insist on either emailing or faxing invoices. Therefore, today when we talk about one centralized location, we mean one snail mail address, one email address and one fax number.

How Automation Helps: With invoice automation, copies of invoices can be sent with a few clicks of a mouse. It is relatively easy to receive invoices either centrally and immediately forward to the appropriate parties or to give both parties (accounts payable and purchasing) online visibility to the invoice.

Challenge: Invoice Volume

Tips in a Paper World: In a paper world, the sheer number of invoices is a concern. As the number increases, it is sometimes necessary to add staff simply to handle the volume. Many organizations look to p-cards to get many small dollar invoices out of accounts payable. Those organizations dealing with numerous small dollar invoices from the same vendor in a short period of time sometimes decide to pay from weekly or monthly statements instead of individual invoices.

How Automation Helps: When invoice processing is automated, volume is less of a concern. The only exception might be for those using software that charges on a per-invoice basis. In those cases, the organization might want to investigate some of the solutions suggested for the paper world.

Challenge: Invoice Routing for Approvals when Approvers Don't Respond

Tips in a Paper World: When invoices are sent out for approval in a paper world, accounts payable does not always know if someone is out on vacation, out unexpectedly or is just not bothering to review the invoices sent. There is no good solution to this problem in a paper world. One partial solution involves developing a list of people known to be negligent in approving invoices and send them regular reminders, perhaps copying their immediate supervisor if they are tardy. This is a bit of work.

How Automation Helps: In an automated world, if approval escalations (sometimes referred to as cascading approvals) are included, the problem goes away. When an invoice is not approved within a preset number of days, the invoice is automatically escalated to the next level for approval. Anecdotal evidence suggests that just including the approval escalation in the process eliminates almost 100% of the tardy approver problem.

Challenge: Tracking Invoices

Tips in a Paper World: Whether you are monitoring invoices out for approval or those that have a dispute "issue," keeping track of invoices can be a real headache in a paper world. We suggest tracking and monitoring disputed invoices using an Excel spreadsheet with regular follow-ups and aging to help identify problem spots as well as get invoice issues addressed.

How Automation Helps: When a fully automated invoice processing system is used, an electronic audit trail is created. Thus, at any point in time, anyone with access can view where an invoice is in the process and who touched it, changed it and when. Additionally, special tracking routines can be built into some third party systems during the initial configuration stage.

Challenge: Dispute resolution

Tips in a Paper World: In a paper world, dispute resolution boils down to phone calls and emails. It's easy for invoices to fall through the cracks if the matter isn't resolved quickly or it is necessary to get additional documentation. Whether in a paper world or in an electronic environment, dispute resolution typically ends up in accounts payable. This is unfortunate as almost always it is necessary to get purchasing or receiving involved to settle the dispute.

How Automation Helps: When dispute resolution is automated, the problem is posted online. Each party is then responsible for checking to see what items are disputed and then resolving their issue. If they don't fulfill their task by an agreed upon deadline, reminders can be automated as well as escalations.

Challenge: Monitoring invoice disputes

Tips in a Paper World: Disputed invoices have a way of disappearing in a paper environment. Unless there is rigorous tracking and follow up, the disputes frequently go unresolved and a second invoice is sent and occasionally paid. If there is no online capability to track invoices with problems, the manager should create an Excel spreadsheet where disputes are tracked and aged. Periodically—ideally weekly—the manager should review the aging and check with the processor responsible for old invoices.

How Automation Helps: If a tracking is built into the invoice processing system, the reports discussed above can be generated automatically and reminders sent. While the manager will still have to get involved from time to time, the amount of management involvement will be diminished. And, of course, they won't have to create the tracking and aging reports. The computer will do it for them.

Paper invoices are here to stay, at least for the time being. Effective managers will deal with the problems they create as part of their overall management function. By recognizing the problems ahead of time, they will be equipped to develop strategies to deal with the headaches created by paper.

CHAPTER 8
OPERATIONAL ISSUES: PAYMENTS

There are a number of operational issues when it comes to payments. In this section we look at a number of the more common ones including:

- Early Payment Discounts
- Rush Checks
- Returning Checks to Requisitioners
- Void Checks
- Late Fees

Early Payment Discounts

Early payment discounts, as our readers are well aware, represent a goldmine for their organizations. Conversely the suppliers who offer them, mainly because it's been part of their business model for decades would love to get rid of them. While most don't go out of their way to openly sabotage your chances of earning these attractive discounts, they don't do anything to make it easier for you either. In this regard, there are two contributions accounts payable can make to their organizations' profitability. They can make sure they don't lose any discounts offered and they can search for additional vendors who offer them. Let's take a look at some strategies that will help you be successful on both fronts.

Earning Every Discount

It's up to you to make sure you do everything possible to make sure you earn every last one of those discounts. Of course, the first step is making sure you receive those invoices as quickly as possible. Then those invoices must be processed quickly. Here's five ways to do that.

- **Tactic #1**: Set up a different PO Box for discount vendors. Of course, the invoices received in this box should be processed before others.

- **Tactic #2**: Try and convince as many of your early discount vendors to send invoices by email or fax. This way you eliminate the mail time and can add that extra two or three days to your processing time.

- **Tactic #3**: Have the invoices from early payment discount vendors flagged when received and then fast track them for processing AND dispute resolution.

- **Tactic #4**: If the invoices are going to purchasing first, make sure the approvers know which vendors' invoices need to be addressed immediately.

- **Tactic #5**: Track all lost early payment discounts and identify root causes for missing the discounts. Periodically review this information and categorize common reasons and reengineer your processes to eliminate them.

Finding More Discounts

Yes, you're not seeing things. We think it is possible for you to find additional discount opportunities for your organization. It won't be easy and there won't be a lot of them. But, we do believe you can find a few. Here's how.

- **Tactic #1**: Instruct your processors to look for notice on every invoice. This includes vendors who don't normally offer you early payment discounts.

Here's why. Occasionally a vendor will offer early payment discounts to a select group of customers. While you'd like to be part of that elite group, it's difficult to join if you don't know about it. Needless to say, the vendor has no interest in letting you know that some of its customers are getting early payment discounts. However, occasionally they slip up and someone inadvertently checks the box that causes the invoice to print the early payment discount terms on the invoice. Once you have it once, you should a) take it immediately and b) notify the appropriate person in purchasing so they can negotiate for it all the time in the future.

- **Tactic #2**: If one vendor in an industry is offering discount terms, ask other vendors in same industry. While collusion on pricing and terms is a definite no-no, it is not uncommon to find all suppliers in the same industry offering very similar if not identical terms. Therefore, if one is offering, ask its competitors. This is a project accounts payable could work on with purchasing.

- **Tactic #3**: If a vendor accepts p-cards and you don't have a program, ask for an early payment discount instead. In fact, consider trying to convert p-card vendors to early payment discount vendors. They may be amenable, especially if you are paying large invoices using the card. In fact, this could benefit both parties. Here's why. While you might be trading part of a rebate for the early payment discount, it is almost a certainty that the early payment discount is larger than your rebate. On the other side of the coin, your vendor can offer you an early payment discount that is smaller than discount fee it is paying its card processor. This is one time when the situation is really a win-win for both parties.

Early payment discounts offer a unique opportunity for all organizations. Make sure you not only earn every one your organization is entitled to but you find those limited situations where additional ones are available.

A Five-Step Plan to Get Rid of Rush Checks

Rush checks, also sometimes referred to as ASAP checks, are those last-minute request for payments that have to be handled outside the normal payment production cycle.

More than an occasional Rush check is often the first sign of a well-run organization with problems in their accounts payable process. If this has you scratching your head, let me explain. Rush checks are one of the leading causes of both duplicate payments and fraud. Plus, they can also get you into trouble on a Sarbanes-Oxley audit if you have too many of them. While everyone understands that no business runs so smoothly that the occasional rush check won't be called for, more than a few each month is a sign that the function is just not running as well as it should.

Why the Fuss?

If fraud and duplicate payments aren't enough to convince you that your organization shouldn't permit rush checks (also sometimes called ASAP checks or manual checks), here are a few more reasons to get rid of them.

1) Rush checks are very expensive to issue when you take into account the time it takes to produce them.

2) Issuing rush checks disrupts the accounts payable function making it less efficient.

3) More than a few rush checks demonstrate poor internal controls.

4) When rush checks are permitted on a regular basis, the rest of the company gets lazy and makes no attempt to avoid them.

5) Rush checks often are sent by overnight delivery making them even more expensive.

The Action Plan

If you want to put a serious dent in the number of rush checks issued in your organization, try the following:

 • Convince management that they really are a bad idea. Use the facts discussed in this article along with some numbers demonstrating just how expensive a rush check actually is.

- **Make it *really* difficult for someone to get a rush check. This could include requiring a sign-off from the CFO** along with an explanation of why this payment could not wait for the regular check cycle. If the CFO is a believer in eliminating rush checks, this step alone may do the trick.

- **Identify the causes for rush checks by keeping a log of who requests them and why.** After you have a few weeks or months activity, you should be able to identify trends and culprits (both at your company and on the outside) and then fix the problem.

- **Identify duplicate payments made with a rush or manual check.** Bring this to the attention of everyone involved and management. There's nothing like seeing a large-dollar amount associated with rush checks to put an end to the practice.

- **Insist on paying electronically instead of by check. When you do get a request for a rush check, insist on ACH payment. Hopefully you will convince the recipient to be paid electronically in the future eliminating them from future rush check pools.**

By relentlessly keeping after the issue and refusing to let it grow you can make some serious headway in reducing the number of those time-wasting, productivity-sucking, rush check requests.

Some Simple Ways to Reduce the Number of Rush Check Requests

It's an old problem; but one that many of our readers still grapple with: the Rush check issue. While Rush checks make for an inefficient payment process and lead to duplicate payments, there is an even more alarming, and often over-looked component to the problem. Rush checks are often returned to the requisitioner so he or she can make the payment personally. This is an internal control concern and one method used by unscrupulous employees to perpetrate fraud. Best practices require that checks be mailed not returned to an employee for hand delivery. So what can you do to reduce the number of Rush checks you issue? Here are three simple tactics that should help.

Talk to the Requester

When approached with a rush check request, which is almost always presented as an emergency, ask a few questions. Find out when the payment is due. If the requestor has the invoice make sure the response matches the information on the invoice. Sometimes people think there is an emergency when there really isn't one. If your check run is in one or two days, ask if the payment can wait a day or two.

Before you turn down someone with a request, find out the real reason the emergency check is needed and what caused the delay. With that information you will be able to make a good business decision regarding the ASAP check.
If you determine management will ultimately overrule your decision not to issue the check, reconsider your refusal. If you want to make a point, go ahead. Otherwise be magnanimous. Take the opportunity to discuss the reasons you dislike rush checks and why it is bad for the organization as a whole.

Insist on Mailing the Payment

Occasionally, the request for the rush check is really just an attempt to get around a no-check-return-to-requestor policy. Once the requester realizes the check will not be returned for delivery but will be mailed, they may back down on their request. Even if they don't, you will not receive future "Rush requests" for phantom reasons. If you have trouble getting management to agree on a No-Return-to-Requisitioner policy, look to your auditors for support. Both your internal and/or external auditors should back you 100% on this issue.

Better Yet, Insist on ACH

Finally, if you have been trying to move the vendor in question to electronic payments without much success, insist the payment be made electronically. When the vendor sees how quickly it gets paid, it may opt to sign on for electronic payments all the time. This is an every-problem-presents-an-opportunity approach. It is also a way to get problematic vendors converted to electronic payments.

While we recognize that Rush checks in all likelihood will never go away completely, these tactics should provide the ammunition to get the number down significantly.

Why Returning Checks Can Be a Problem

Checks should not be returned to requestors for two simple reasons: it's inefficient and it opens the door to fraud. I could write a million words explaining the inconveniences to accounts payable caused by requests to return checks and it might make some impact on a few. I could write about the potential for fraud in theory and more but it would have half the effect one of our readers does with a real-life tale. Here is the story in the professional's words.

"A former employee, who was in charge of all the tradeshow planning, would request checks to be processed, payable to the tradeshows. The request was approved by the same person using the initials of their superior. This was common practice at that time, due to the lengthy traveling the superior does. Now when I think about it, how stupid were we to put that much trust in someone? We have a list of people allowed to sign the checks here, none are stamped.

Those individuals signed these checks, trusting the former employee, and allowed me to return the checks to her believing they were getting sent to the tradeshows. Five years into the situation, one of the VP's decided to find out why the tradeshows were costing so much. We found out why. This ordeal cost the company a lot of money. Since then we have drastically changed our policies. *I will not give any check back to the requester.* The only exception are specific requests signed off by an officer of the company."

This story emphasizes, once again, the old adage about fraud being committed by long-term trusted employees. If you are still getting nowhere on this issue, you can always point out that under Sarbanes-Oxley, returning checks to requisitioners could be considered poor internal controls.

There are also practical considerations as explained by another reader, whose company does allow the return of checks to employees. This professional explains that "Many times the check never gets mailed out to the vender. Then AP gets a call wondering where payment is. When we research this we find out the departments pick up the check and forget to mail out the check."

An End Run around the Problem

Getting as many vendors as possible set up for ACH payment helps. This way there is no check to return and the confrontation with the requestor is avoided. Now some might point out that this does not address the underlying issue within the company, but it does avoid some of the battles and allows accounts payable to chip away at the problem, especially if management isn't willing to back a "no-return-to-requisitioner policy."

Here's another way to make ACH work for you in this regard. If certain employees routinely demand that checks be returned to them for particular vendors, and management allows it, consider recruiting the vendor in question for participation in your ACH program. Once you've got the vendor on board for ACH, you can even tell the requestor that the vendor prefers payment this way. (By the way, used in the earlier trade show example, this approach would have uncovered the fraud.)

Need Checks Returned: Here's a Policy You Can Use

One of the semi-legitimate reasons employees ask for a check to be returned to them is that they need to attach it to some other material. This may be a conference registration, a subscription form or something like that.
While we are loathe to recommend anything that will add to the administrative burden in accounts payable, this is one time when, alas, that is what we are going to do.

Set up a process that allows employees to send along material that must be included with the check and then make it part of the check mailing process that these items be reattached to the check prior to the mailing.

You can also try talking to employees who want their checks returned to find out the reason behind these requests.

Sometimes you will be able to suggest an acceptable alternative. For example, occasionally an executive needs a check to present to a charitable organization. We've all seen the televised events with the executive presenting a huge facsimile of a check. You can create a similar, albeit not so large, reproduction for your executives to use.

By imaginatively addressing the problem, forward-thinking professionals will be able to minimize the number of checks returned to requisitioners in their organizations.

Void Checks: To Save or Not to Save

When it comes to voided checks there are two schools of thought. The first group advocates for destroying the paper while the second believes in carefully voiding the check and saving them. Each group makes a good point. We come down on the side of saving the items and we'll explain why. But, first let's look at the problems each approach presents.

The Void Check Headache

For starters, let's point out that you do not always have the paper check that represents a void item. Often items are voided because the customer hasn't received payment and a new check has to be issued. In these cases, a stop payment is issued at the bank and the transaction reversed in the accounting system. Once a check has been voided and reversed on your financial records the problem is what to do with the paper check, assuming you have it.

Those who recommend shredding and discarding the paper check believe that saving it is a waste of time and space and represents a risk to the organization. The risk is that someone will get hold of the voided check and use it or the information on it to commit fraud. The group that believes in saving the checks also raise a good point. When the auditors want to see proof that a payment wasn't made twice, your possession of that voided check makes the point. There is also the unclaimed property issue.

Void checks are often requested during an unclaimed property audit, she says. Every check that is issued is considered "unclaimed" property until it is cashed, unless you can prove that the debt that it originally represented was settled in another manner. Voiding a check creates the need to show "why" to an unclaimed property auditor, so it's good to keep the actual checks, if possible, to prove a legitimate business process and intention when avoiding checks (to disprove the auditor's assumption that you void them just to attempt to prevent them from being "outstanding" for escheat purposes).

Best Practice

While we can see the validity of both sides, the unclaimed property audit concern outweighs the logic of shredding – at least to our mind.

> 1)   Document, document, document – everything you do.
>
> 2)   Void the check by writing void across the face and removing the signature line
>
> 3)   Keep a log and the originals in a secure location
>
> Readers should note that the whole messy issue of void checks is avoided if they move to electronic payments.

Late Fees

Late fees are the fees that some vendors charge their customers for payments not received by the due date. While most readers probably are aware of this issue from their personal dealings, it can be an issue for some firms despite the fact that most have a policy of never paying late fees.

To be honest, few vendors actively chase late fees. They simply accrue them on their books. Some will collect them eventually, if a vendor has an open credit that goes unclaimed for too long.

CHAPTER 9
INACCURATE PAYMENTS AND PAYMENT AUDITING

Alas, virtually every organization makes a duplicate or improper payment at some point. While it would be nice if the vendor receiving the over-payment would return it, but as those with even a modicum of experience in the accounts payable arena are painfully aware, that rarely happens. Therefore it is imperative that all organizations making payments take some steps to review their payment activity and recover inaccurate or excess payments. In this chapter, we look at:

- Routines for identifying duplicate payments

- Performing your own payment audit to recover funds before a third party is engaged

- Hiring a recovery firm

Duplicate Payment Avoidance Best Practices

Duplicate and erroneous payments are a continuing plague of every accounts payable function. While a few will always sneak through, there are steps every organization should be taking to keep that amount to a bare minimum. While some of the basic prevention techniques have stayed the same, some no longer work. What's more, to be completely effective, it is imperative that every organization introduce new procedures to address the frustratingly new problems that seem to arise any time we change practices. What follows are 20 steps every organization should be employing to handle the duplicate and erroneous payment issue.

1. A written policy and procedures manual detailing exactly how invoices should be processed is the first line of defense against duplicate payments. It should be regularly reviewed and updated. Give it to all processors so they can refer to it, if they have a question.

2. Train all processors thoroughly making sure each understands every facet of the job. Periodically retrain if you suspect something has been forgotten or a new procedure is introduced. It is critical that all processors use the exact same procedures.

3. Periodically check to make sure all your processors are still following the procedures as detailed in your policy and procedures manual. When processors introduce their own shortcuts, they unintentionally set the stage for duplicate payments.

4. Create a detailed coding standard for invoice data entry and make sure all processors use it exactly as it is written.

5. Create a naming convention for master vendor file data entry that matches your invoice coding standards. Again, it should be used exactly as written, no shortcuts allowed.

6. Employ strong master vendor file practices across the board. For if they are ignored, duplicate payments will creep in.

7. Require your suppliers include an invoice number on all invoices. Invoices that do not have an invoice number should be returned with a polite letter explaining this requirement. This condition should be explained to all new vendors before they submit the first invoice.

8. Likewise, it is not unreasonable to require that all invoices show a PO number or the name of the requisitioner on them. Do not waste time trying to figure out who ordered something, if the invoice is missing this crucial piece of information. Simply return it with a polite letter saying this information is

required in order to get all vendors paid on a timely basis.

9. Paying on time greatly reduces the number of second invoices submitted by vendors looking for payment. It is those second invoices that cause a good portion of those unwanted duplicate payments.

10.	Whenever an item is submitted for a Rush payment, do a little extra research to ensure the item hasn't already been paid. What's more, keep a file of these items and double check 30 or 60 days later to ensure the original invoice didn't show up and end up getting paid.

11.	When an invoice shows up for payment long after its due date, do a little extra research to make sure it hasn't been paid. Don't forget to check that Rush folder that has copies of items recently paid on a Rush basis, perhaps without all the normal backup.

12.	The newest problem for those accepting electronic invoices are those vendors who in their zeal to ensure you get their invoice, email and snail mail the invoice. Identify and educate those vendors to the fact that they don't need to send the invoice by snail mail.

13.	Centralize the receipt of invoices, ideally in accounts payable, so they can be tracked and processed in a timely manner. This also helps when a vendor calls to see if an invoice has been received. If accounts payable can answer affirmatively, they won't feel the need to send another copy.

14.	Do a little extra research before paying large invoices. The reason for this is that while all duplicate payments are troublesome, double paying a large invoice really hurts financially. Of course, each organization will have its own definition of large.

15.	In an ideal world, each vendor would be able to be paid with only one payment vehicle (check, ACH, p-card or wire). However, most don't have this luxury. Pay extra attention to invoices from vendors that can be paid with more than one payment vehicle.

16. When payments are made outside accounts payable, make sure the folks making those payments employ the same rigid processing standards used in accounts payable. This means they must use the same rigid coding standards, perform the three way match and extinguish the purchase order and receiving document once the payment has been made. This is more likely to happen with ACH payments and wire transfers.

17. Some organizations go the extra mile and routinely run all ACH and wires against their check register to identify potential duplicate transactions. They also take the list of all transactions paid for with p-cards and run them against the check register looking for possible duplicates

18. Create an internal pre or post payment review team. Ideally, this will be done before the payments are made but practically speaking this is not always possible. While doing it after the fact isn't as valuable, it still should be done.

19. Once you've done everything you can, call in the pros and let them look for duplicate and erroneous payments. They will give you a management report when they are finished. Closely review their results and make any adjustments to your processes needed to close any weak spots that were allowing duplicate payments to be made.

20. Realize the quest to prevent duplicate and erroneous payments is an ongoing process. Even if you have an ironclad process today, there's always the chance that things will change and money will slip through the corporate fingers in the form of duplicates. Continuously review your processes and look for new problem areas. With a little luck, they will be few and far between. However, there is one thing that is certain: at some point there will be a new problem you'll have to address.

Recover the Easy Overpayments Yourself before Hiring a Payment Auditor

Whenever the topic of payment recovery auditors is raised over half the people in the room put on their No-Way-Jose face. They argue that the auditors charge too much or recover funds they could easily get back themselves—if they had the time. And therein lies the problem. No one is denying that savvy AP professionals couldn't find and recover a good deal of the duplicate and erroneous payments on their own but many don't. The problem is simply one of too much work and not enough time to go after the low hanging fruit. So in the end, many organizations leave that money with their vendors and it is never recovered. As most reading this are ever so painfully aware, only a few vendors return duplicate payments or voluntarily provide information about outstanding credits.

Accounts Payable Now & Tomorrow strongly advocates the use of recovery auditors working on a contingency basis. That being said, we do understand the reluctance to pay someone to recover funds that are easily identified. We recommend that readers with limited resources to devote to a payment recovery project pursue the three items discussed below – and then call a contingency auditor to get the rest for them.

The States

Probably the easiest funds to find are those that have been turned over to the states in your name. Now, before you get on this bandwagon, let us warn you that this comes with a huge caveat. Only take this step if you are currently reporting and remitting your unclaimed property to the states. If you are not, your inquiry could very well trigger an audit which is likely to result in a larger payment to the states than what you will receive back from them.

If in compliance, go to www.missingmoney.com and look for funds in your organization's name as well as any DBAs and abbreviations or variances that your suppliers may use. When you find funds, fill out the requisite paperwork and wait. Given the current fiscal pressures, some states are taking a bit of time to return funds to their rightful owners.

The caveat also applies to work done on your behalf by auditors. If you are not in compliance or simply prefer not to deal with the states, instruct your auditors not to go after funds held by the states. Some do this as a matter of course so make sure you discuss the matter with them.

Deposits

If your accounting system is capable of generating a list of all deposits given in the last ten years, analyze the list and determine which should have been returned. It is possible some of the older deposits were turned over to the states. Once you've identified the deposits no longer needed, go after them.

Now, when some think about deposits, they only think about rental real estate. But there are many other places deposits may be required. These include the post office, some telecom services, leases of some computer and photocopying equipment and other items.

If your system is not capable of generating such a list, start tracking deposits so you can retrieve them in the future.

Vendor Credits

Many vendors routinely send out customer statements. Many of these same vendors routinely suppress the inclusion of outstanding credits on these statements. I'm willing to bet that most of the vendors who pull this trick do not turn the open credits over to the state at the requisite time, either.

Request vendor statements from all vendors. Emphasize to the vendor that you'd like them to include all activity not just open invoices. Otherwise, it is an exercise in futility. When you locate the open credits, collect them. Some vendors like to insist that you use the credits to purchase more goods from them. Unless there is something in your terms and conditions that dictates this, they have no legal right to demand an additional purchase.

Ideally, you should request the open credits be sent to you separate from any invoice you are paying. The reason for this is to create a clear audit trail. If you use them to reduce an existing invoice payment make sure you document what you do. This way, should the supplier claim that you did not pay them in full at some point down the road, you will have the necessary documentation to prove otherwise.

There are several vendors who will go after vendor credits for you at a rate lower than their contingency fee for other types of recoveries. Should you not have the staff to handle this task for you, negotiate with a auditor to handle it for you.

Once you have collected everything you possibly can on your own, it's time to call in the big guns. Without them the money is gone forever. Better to pay someone to recover it for you and add something to your bottom line than to do nothing and get nothing in return.

Benefits of an Overpayment Audit: It's Not Only about the Money

When most organizations undertake an overpayment recovery audit, clearly they are focused on the funds that have been paid in error. These recoveries might be duplicate payments discounts not taken, or a variety of erroneous invoiced charges. But, the recoveries, however attractive they may be, are just the beginning of the benefits accruing to an organization savvy enough to commission an overpayment audit.

The fact that overpayment audits are typically conducted on a contingency basis means that no budget is required to get one started. This relieves most controllers and CFOs of the onerous task of finding the funds. And since the only costs involved generally are the contingency amount to the audit firm, 100% the money then disbursed to the organization can go right to the bottom line. That's something that warms the hearts of even the coldest financial executives.

Beyond the hard dollars auditors also can:

- Identify weak spots in your processes that need to be addressed.

- Find the occasional fraud, which you can take action against.

- Recommend process improvements to prevent overpayments in the future.

The specialty auditors (advertising, telecom, freight etc.) bring industry-specific knowledge to the table enabling them to identify overpayments that would not be recovered without that insider perspective. Anyone who has ever taken a close look at the details associated with a large advertising contract or even a straight telecom bill knows that unless you know exactly what you are looking for, the vendor could pile on excess charges and you would never realize it.

Finally—and this may be difficult to swallow if it turns out to be the case in your situation—the auditors may find that certain vendors have been taking advantage of you for years. Do you want to continue doing business with them?

Overpayments audits not only make good business sense, they are a recommended best practice for any organization interested in bottom-line profitability and strong internal controls.

Questions to Ask when Hiring a Payment Recovery Audit Firm

The last line of defense in the war against duplicate payments is to hire a duplicate payment audit firm, also referred to as a recovery audit firm, to find those duplicates that slithered through your highly guarded payment fortress. While no organization likes to admit they make duplicate payments, even those employing every best practice imaginable do let one or two slip through. When you get ready to hire a firm, these 20 questions shown in the accompanying table will help you narrow the field and select the recovery group best suited to your company.

References

While there is no right or wrong answer to any of the questions asked, the responses will help you form a picture of the audit firm and how it will mesh with your organization. Be sure to ask for references from all firms you are considering hiring but take those references with a huge grain of salt. Few will offer references from jobs that did not go well or where the client wasn't satisfied.

If you belong to an industry group, ask at your regional meetings for both recommendations and names of firms where the audits have not gone well. But, remember, occasionally a job doesn't go well because the company in question cannot or does not provide the information the auditors need to conduct a satisfactory audit.

The Hourly Rate vs. Contingency fee Debate

Expect a huge conversation when you ask if the employees of the firm work on an hourly rate or a contingency fee. This is a hotly contested issue in the industry with strong feelings on both sides.

The main issue, as you might imagine, is that when folks are paid on a contingency basis, they are less likely to aggressively pursue small dollar transactions. This is where the bulk of the duplicate payments are likely to occur when viewed from a number of transactions basis – but not where the lion's share of the recovered dollars are.

The Consultants' Report

Most good audit firms will provide a report at the end of the engagement that identifies the weaknesses in your processes that allowed the duplicates to slip through. This is extremely valuable and should be used to fix your processes. Remember it comes from an unbiased third party.

Unfortunately, many of the auditors I speak to reveal – off the record, of course – that their clients rarely take the actions they recommend. This provides another earning opportunity for the auditor a year or two down the road.

Insist on getting the report and then use it to reduce duplicate payments in the future. Often it contains advice you have already been cautioned about, either from your staff or accountants, but have not implemented. It will also improve your Sarbanes-Oxley compliance.

Once the decision to hire a firm has been made, use the questions in the accompanying table to help you select the firm that best meets your needs – and then don't forget to follow the advice they give in their Consultant's Report.

20 Questions to Help You Select the Perfect Recovery Firm

1. Do they have experience in your industry? Industry experience, while not crucial, is desirable as the auditors arrive knowing which vendors are likely to cause duplicate payments.

2. Will the firm provide a report at the end showing the weaknesses in your process? This should be a requirement for any firm you consider hiring. For without this report, you are only getting half of what you paid for – and are likely to continue making the same mistakes over and over again.

3. Does the agency work on a contingency fee or hourly rate? There is no right or wrong answer to this

question. It is mostly a matter of what you are comfortable with.

4. What is the smallest recovery they pursue? While it is not realistic to expect the auditors to pursue every last dollar, those with high thresholds should be viewed with some caution unless you make very few small dollar payments. For most organizations, a threshold of $250 - $500 is reasonable.

5. Will they reduce their rates for large recoveries? While most organizations are willing to pay a 25% recovery fee for a $500 duplicate payment, they are not willing to pay that on a $500,000 duplicate. In fact, this is the issue that prevents many people from hiring a recovery firm in the first place. Ask for a reduction in fees. While most won't offer it, if asked they will comply.

6. How much can you expect to receive based on their experience with organizations similar to yours? Of course the answer to this should be taken with a huge grain of salt. There is no real way to know. Unless you have very poor controls in place, the answer should be around .5%, i.e. $5,000 per $1,000,000 of payables. Obviously, those with good controls will have a lower number.

7. How long has the audit firm been in business? If the answer is low, ask how long the principals have been in the industry. They will probably offer this information if they have not been in business for that long. This is not necessarily a bad thing, for they may be willing to take a lower recovery fee than those organizations with a big roster of clients.

8. How many full-time employees does it have? This is an indicator of the quality of people who are likely to work your account. If the audit firm routinely hires temps, your recoveries may not be as high as they would under different circumstances.

9. Are the employees paid on a contingency or hourly rate? There is no right or wrong answer to this question. While those paid on a contingency basis are more likely to focus on your higher dollar items, they are also likely to be more aggressive.

10.   What is the background of the principals of the organization? This will give you an idea of their understanding of the industry. It is important that they have worked in the industry or related industries for a good deal of time. If not, they should have some very senior employees who have.

11.   What is the background of the employees who will work your case? You want at least one or two experienced professionals on your account. You do not want to be the organization given a bunch of temps because the audit firm took on more clients than it could handle. This doesn't happen often, but it does on occasion.

12.   If you have a lot of freight, advertising, utility billings, postage, telecom billings, ask if the firm has specialized experience in those arenas. These areas involve extreme minutia and as such, specialized knowledge. Expect to pay more for these audits than you would a straight accounts payable duplicate payment audit. Get references and inquire about the background of the people who will work your case.

13.   How much of your staff time will be taken up with the audit? Most recovery audit firms take very little of your staff time, but some is generally required. Find out ahead of time so you don't end up with poor recoveries because you did not allocate adequate staff to help where needed.

14.   Will the audit firm need office space in your location or is the bulk of the work done offsite?

15.   What are the technical capabilities of the firm? Much of the analytical work is done today using technology. This helps the firm identify potential duplicates quickly and focus on the recovery work. Have some discussion around this topic to determine the level of technical expertise you are hiring.

16.   Will the audit firm do second audits? Each audit firm uses its own proprietary routines to identify duplicates. Few can find them all. It would just take too long. Thus, for large firms, a second audit is recommended.

17. What are your rates for secondary audits? Expect the rates for the secondary audit to be higher, perhaps as much as 50%. This is because the cream, or easy finds, has been taken by the primary audit. Make sure to tell the secondary auditor who did your primary audit. There is a very good reason for this. They auditors know who uses routines similar to their own – and hence, know where they will do a good audit and where they won't. Respect their decision not to pursue and audit when you tell them who did your primary audit.

18. How/when does the firm expect to be paid? Does it expect payment when it identifies the duplicate or when you are actually credited for the amount owed? Obviously, you do not want to pay the audit firm until you have either been paid or issued a credit by your vendors.

19. If you decide not to pursue a duplicate (which you might for a variety of reasons) does the auditor still expect to be compensated? Technically, they have a right to be paid but many will defer if pursuing the duplicate might put you in an embarrassing position – say pursuing a duplicate from a company owned by someone on your Board of Directors.

20. How long does the auditor expect the audit to take and when can they start? This information will help you plan for any staffing and space requirements. Also, if you need the recoveries within a certain fiscal period, it is crucial you select a firm that can meet your time constraints.

CHAPTER 10
EXPENSE REIMBURSEMENT
(TRAVEL AND ENTERTAINMENT)

The travel and entertainment (T&E) reimbursement process has changed considerably in the last few years. It seems like only yesterday that travelers regularly obtained approval from their supervisors for trips beforehand. Although still done in a few organizations, most no longer require it. Cash advances, also once commonplace, are also no longer used at the majority of organizations.

Expense reimbursements for employee travel and entertainment can be complex. In this book we simply present some of the basic components. We'll take a look at:

- The Travel Policy
- Enforcement
- The IRS and the Accountable Plan Status
- Receipts
- Checking
- Reimbursement practices (including per-diems)
- Fraud

The Travel and Entertainment (T&E) Policy Manual

Every organization should have a travel and entertainment policy manual that:

- Is updated regularly, at least once a year;

- Covers every possible eventuality a traveler may encounter;

- Is readily accessible to anyone who may need it; and

- Is sponsored by (or goes out under the signature of) a high-level executive.

Most importantly, and sadly this happens only about 80% of the time, the policy should be enforced uniformly. Rank should not have its privileges. Everyone should be held to the same policy with no exception what so ever.

The T&E policy should spell out the guidelines for company employees when it comes to travel and entertainment. It details some or all of the following:

- What receipts are required

- What is allowable

- What is not allowable

- How documentation should be submitted

- What approvals are necessary

- Timing of reporting

- If cash advances are permitted and, if so, under what circumstances

- If corporate T&E cards must be used

- Reimbursement policy

- What hotel chains are preferred or required

- What airlines are preferred or required

- What car rental agencies are recommended or required

- Whether employees must stay over on a Saturday night if a lower fare can be obtained

- How unused tickets are to be handled

Occasionally organizations are lax when it comes to documenting what's allowed and what's not. They assume their employees have good common sense and wouldn't put something ridiculous through on their expense reports. While this might be true for 95% of your employees, every organization has a few who push the envelope.

So, in order to avoid those "no one ever told me we weren't allowed to" excuses, spell out the policy in as much detail as you can muster.

Policy Enforcement

In theory, when an expense account report and reimbursement request is sent down to accounts payable approved by the appropriate manager, accounts payable should merely pay the reimbursement. Unfortunately in many organizations, policy compliance falls on the shoulders of the accounts payable group although they don't have any real authority to enforce it.

The reality is that few managers actually check the T&E reports submitted by their subordinates. They merely approve whatever is put in front of them. The reasons for this are numerous and largely irrelevant to this discussion. The bottom line is that most expense reports are not checked or verified by the person who puts their signature on the approval line.

The policy should contain statements about managerial responsibility and a decision should be made internally about whether accounts payable is expected to check for policy compliance. Most companies do want their accounts payable group to check for policy compliance because they recognize that their managers are not doing it. If you make that decision, make sure that you back the managers who enforce the policy—because they are anything but popular when they do it.

Of course, an easy way around this issue is to use one of the nifty models on the market today that incorporate a policy compliance feature. Many of these refuse to let employees enter an item that is outside the policy. This takes the onus off both the approving manager and the accounts payable staff. However, at this juncture, many companies are still relying on their staff to check for policy compliance.

There is a growing move to make managers responsible for what they approve. This means that there would be consequences should they approve something that was clearly inappropriate or fraudulent. While we are not suggesting that a manager be fired for failing to monitor and employee's travel expenditures properly, we do recommend that this lapse be taken into account at the time of the annual review. More than a few organizations have implemented this practice.

The IRS and the Accountable Plan Status

The Holy Grail for most organizations reimbursing employees for travel expenditures is their 'Accountable Plan' status with the IRS. If you reimburse all or part of your employees' travel and entertainment expenses, how you reimburse your employees determines the way your company and your employees must treat these reimbursements for income-tax purposes. Reimbursements made to employees under an accountable plan are not subject to payroll or income-tax withholding, but reimbursements paid under non-accountable plans are reported as employee compensation.

Accountable Plan Status

An accountable plan is one that pays for business-related out-of-town lodging, meal expenses and business entertainment expenses on a dollar-for-dollar basis. Reimbursements for these expenditures can be made through cash advances, direct reimbursements to the employee or charges to a company charge card.

To be considered an accountable plan by the IRS, your reimbursement plan must contain each of the following three elements:

1. Reimbursed expenses must have a clear business connection
2. They must have been incurred by your employees

3. The must have been incurred while the employee was performing services on your behalf.

Your employees must adequately account for their expenses within a reasonable period of time (see the definition below). That means they are required to submit documentary evidence of their travel, mileage, and other employee business expenses, along with a statement of expense, an account book, a diary or a similar record in which expenses are entered.

The employee must give you the same type of records and supporting information that they would have to give to the IRS if the IRS questioned an employee business expense deduction on the return of an employee whose employer doesn't have an accountable plan. For business travel, that means a written record of the departure and return dates, trip destination, trip purpose, and amount spent on travel expenses. Receipts must be kept for all lodging and other expenses of $75 or more.

Please note that while the IRS sets a requirement for receipts at $75, you can select a lower dollar amount, if you choose. Most organizations do. In fact, there has been a trend towards lowering the receipt requirement threshold.

Employees must return any excess payments (if a cash advance has been made) within a reasonable period of time. An excess payment is any amount paid to an employee that exceeds the expenses accounted for by the employee. Also, keep in mind that offering cash advances is generally not considered a good practice.

Employees can also be given a flat per diem or daily rate for out-of-town travel no matter what the employee actually spends for lodging, meals, and incidental expenses. If the per-diem allowance does not exceed government-approved rates, employee record-keeping requirements are minimal. Employees just have to submit a written report or statement indicating when and where T&E expenses were incurred, but need not submit bills and receipts.

Receipts

There's a seismic shift going on in the business world and it revolves around how companies are substantiating requests for reimbursement of travel and entertainment expenses. For a long time, most companies required receipts for all expenditures in excess of $25, despite the fact the IRS only required receipts for expenditures more than $75. A new study just completed by AP Now reveals this requirement has gotten more stringent.

Overall Conclusions

As you can see from the table following, almost 60% of the almost 200 respondents now require receipts for all expenditures – regardless of the dollar amount involved. The second most common required level was the expected $25. However, the number of companies using that level was significantly lower than those requiring receipts for everything.

Receipt Requirements for Reimbursement: Total Group

- We require all receipts 58.90%
- $5   0.61%
- $10   1.23%
- $25   26.38%
- $75   3.68%
- Other   9.20%

Does This Mean More Work?

At first glance it might appear that if all receipts are required, there'd be a lot more work in accounts payable. But, this does not have to be if the organization:

1) Relies on managers to check all expense reports before they approve them, and
2) Processors spot check receipts rather than checking every last one.

Best practice organizations that spot check expense reports effectively typically check:

- 5-10% of all reports selected randomly plus
- Reports of known offenders who regularly push the envelope and
- Reports of all C-level executives

By employing the best practice checking routines described above, the amount of work does not have to increase substantially simply because receipts are required for all reimbursement requests.

Is Getting All Receipts Overkill?

At first glance it might seem ridiculous to require all receipts. Can't employees be trusted? The answer, unfortunately, is apparently many can't be. Respondents to our survey were asked to provide examples of ridiculous reimbursement requests. We expected a few amusing stories. We were horrified to find stories from almost all the 200 respondents. In fact only three said they nothing to share.

Here are just a few samples:

- An employee had their car detailed while at long-term parking at the airport.

- Request to reimburse for parking ticket.

- We are located in Florida. Someone went to a northern clime and requested reimbursement for a coat.

- An employee took her entire family along (spouse + three children) on a business trip (without the company's knowledge). She turned in receipts for groceries, meals, a larger vehicle (mini-van) to accommodate all of them and other incidental charges.

Some may make the point that the dollar amount involved in lots of the T&E disputes are small and it is a waste of resources to track them down. There are two answers to that claim. First, fraud is fraud and if permitted will only lead to bigger fraud. And secondly, many larger frauds were uncovered because the fraudster could not resist dipping his or her hand into the T&E pot. When the T&E fraud was investigated, the larger fraud was uncovered.

It appears that we are heading for an era of increased scrutiny in the expense reimbursement arena. Not only is the IRS snooping around but it appears companies are suspicious as well. Employ the best practices when it comes to checking receipts to ensure that this increased scrutiny does not yield a pile of additional work for accounts payable.

Change in T&E Receipt Requirements when Asking for Expense

You would expect that companies changing their receipt requirements for expense reimbursements would raise the dollar level where receipts are required. New research from Accounts Payable & Tomorrow shows just the reverse. Very few are taking that action. What's more, quite a few are asking for more details. Let's take a look at what the survey revealed.

Changes Being Considered for T&E Receipts

While half of our respondents aren't considering changing the receipt level, the other half are. This in and of itself is significant because it signals that many organizations are looking at the issue. While the IRS only requires receipts for expenditures in excess of $75, very few companies have followed their lead. Most use a lower dollar level. When evaluating the numbers below, please keep in mind that almost 60% require receipts for everything, regardless of the dollar level

Action Being Considered	% Considering
Increasing the level where receipts are required	6.79%
Decreasing the level where receipts are required	3.09%
Requiring a detailed receipt for meals showing exactly what was ordered	26.54%
None of the above	50.62%
Other please explain	12.96%

We were intrigued to learn what other changes readers were considering and we thought you would be too. They are:

1)   Itemized receipts required when eating with others.

2)   Requiring additional receipts for charged items. Credit card statements are sometimes vague.

3)   Per Diems. It should be noted that a number of respondents reported they were considering this move. The beauty of it is it eliminates lots of checking and other issues.

4)   Having lower thresholds for receipts for newly hired employees.

5)   Detailed receipts for meals.

6)   We are looking at both a per diem option and also requiring the itemized meal receipt.

The Ugly Issue

In some organizations there is concern over employees eating an inexpensive meal and then putting in a reimbursement request just under the level where a receipt is required. We asked respondents if this is a concern in their organization.

Keep in mind, that almost 60% are already requiring a receipt for everything. Even with that, 25.31% are troubled by this issue.

The Even Uglier Issue

Lastly we asked respondent, if you are willing to share, how their organization treated inappropriate expense reimbursement requests. Whether it's the impact of a poor economy, a better understanding of how poor expense reimbursement habits hurt the bottom line or a fear of the IRS is not clear. But, overwhelmingly the tide seems to be turning. Finally, there appears to be overwhelming management support when it comes to dealing with questionable expense reimbursement requests.

We had over 100 responses to this question so we'll summarize to some extent. The most common response was that the expense was simply denied. One participant summed it up this way; "One word...no!"

Some simply took it off the expense report and reimbursed at the lower amount while others sent it back asking the traveler to resubmit. Many copied the traveler's supervisor when they took this action. The next common approach was to return the offending report to the supervisor who had approved the item asking about it. There were many variations on how this is done, but here's one explanation that was typical of our respondents. "The expense report form is returned to the manager who approved it with a copy of the company policy & procedure for expense reporting. A brief note on what the issue is would be noted."

Referencing the travel policy is a common tactic even for those who deny the reimbursement request outright. Many noted how they were able to do this because they have a strong travel policy <u>and</u> are backed by management on this issue. Additionally, many counsel the employee.

Why Some Companies Are Starting to Get Meal Receipts

Processing and auditing travel and entertainment expense reimburse requests is tedious enough without adding another step. But that is exactly what some organizations are starting to do. They are requiring the meal receipt that shows exactly what was ordered. While a few companies have been doing this for years, most haven't. What follows is a short list of the reasons why these receipts are sometimes requested and then a discussion on the best way to handle this additional influx of paper (or hopefully images to be audited).

The Rationale

If you are scratching your head wondering why receipts are being requested, consider the following.

1) If your organization has grants that prohibit the use of the funds to pay for alcohol, you might want require this additional documentation. Additionally, a few companies do not reimburse for liquor for individual meals so they might also wish to monitor. By the way, this is not to say that your employees cannot have a drink with their meals. They simply must pay for it themselves. This means either requesting a separate bill or deducting the amount from the reimbursement. In an era when organizations need to keep costs under control,

making sure that spending outside the approved policy does not occur is one way to rein in expenses.

2) A few other organizations check these meal receipts to figure out how many people attended the event. While this might seem intrusive to some, there is actually some logic behind this, especially if you suspect that some employees are routinely adding people to an event who having nothing to do with the business. And, that is to make sure you are in compliance with all IRS regulations related to your accountable plan status. As you may recall, one of the requirements for reporting expenses to the IRS is that the name and business relationship be listed for every attendee at an event (including meals the company pays for).

3) Then there is the latest scam being used by a very few employees to bilk their organization for money they are not entitled to. Here's how it goes. An employee takes someone out to a business lunch. They fully report the event, meeting IRS documentation requirements. However, before they pay the bill at the restaurant, they have the restaurant include a gift card intended for personal use – not as a gift to a vendor or customer. It is unlikely this can be determined from the receipt – unless the itemized receipt is requested. Requiring the itemized receipt will serve as a deterrent. Hopefully none of your employees would be foolish enough to commit this fraud and then turn in the receipt showing the gift card. So, if you move to this requirement, do not expect to see gift cards showing up on the receipts.

Monitoring These Receipts

Now if you are thinking "uggh, more tedious work for the department" fear not. While you might require these receipts and the organization's employees might believe they are all being checked, you should not devote too much time to that task. If your policy makes managers responsible for the T&E expense reimbursement reports they approve and really does hold them accountable if they don't, you will not have much additional work. Spot check these receipts. This means looking at maybe five to ten percent of these receipts and perhaps looking at the receipts of those employees known to take liberty with their entertainment budgets.

Checking/Auditing T&E Reports

It simply isn't cost effective for most companies to check every report and every receipt. The cost involved with such in-depth checking versus the amount of money saved is usually excessive—the dollar chasing a dime principle. Therefore, it is now considered a best practice to only spot check T&E reports. Typically reports are selected for checking:

- Randomly;
- If they exceed policy guidelines in any area;
- If the total expenses on the report exceed a certain pre-assigned level; and
- If the individual has been identified as one whose reports have been questionable in the past.

Companies that spot check, audit anywhere from 5-25% of their employees' reports. Typically, when a company moves to a spot check process, they start at the 25% level and as the company gains comfort with the process it progressively checks a smaller and smaller number until 5 or 10% are being monitored.

Reimbursement Practices

The reimbursement of funds paid out of the employee's pocket is the carrot that helps organizations get T&E reports completed on a timely basis. Some—OK, many—employees dislike filling out their reimbursement reports. In some organizations, especially those that issue company-paid credit cards, getting the reports turned in on time can be a real problem.

Ideally, once the reports are turned in and approved by the supervisor of the traveling employee, they are sent to accounts payable for final review and reimbursement. Once the report has been verified the employee should be reimbursed by an electronic payment to his or her bank account. Alternatively, it can be included with payroll, although most payroll departments prefer to avoid this.

It should be noted that the filing, review, and approval are either done on paper or electronically. The filing method does not affect the reimbursement approach.

Recommended Approach

It is strongly recommended that the department responsible for travel and entertainment (usually accounts payable but sometimes payroll or, at larger companies, a separate T&E unit) publish a schedule letting employees know the deadlines for T&E submission if they want payment at certain times. By making this schedule readily available to all travelers some of the problems with late submissions are avoided.

There are very few things more unpleasant for a manager than dealing with an angry employee who missed a filing deadline and now has to pay a large credit card bill out of his or her own pocket.

Second Best Approach

Alternatively, if payments are not made electronically, checks can be mailed to the employees' homes. Having checks handed out by a processor is time consuming, inefficient, and leads to all kinds of other problems (fraud, lost checks etc.).

The problem for many organizations is that there are a few employees who will demand a paper check and do not want it mailed home. Typically, although they will not tell you this, the reason is they are hiding income from a spouse or partner. This is an age-old problem that continues to this day.

Without offering an opinion on employee motives, it's fair to say that no organization should be put in the position where they are asked to utilize inefficient processes simply to meet employees' personal objectives that have nothing to do with the organization's core mission.

Reimbursing by paper check picked up by hand is a poor use of an organization's valuable resources and is considered a poor internal control.

Per-Diems

Many organizations using per diems to reimburse employees for employment-related travel base their reimbursement rates on the data provided by the U.S. General Services Administration (GSA). This is especially true if you do business with the government. If your organization falls into this category you'll need to use the new recently released numbers.

Per diems are a daily allowance for lodging (excluding taxes), meals, and incidental expenses for traveling employees. The GSA establishes the maximum CONUS (continental United States). Per Diem rates for federal travel customers are reviewed annually. The current maximum CONUS rates are provided as part of Appendix A of Chapter 301 of the Federal Travel Regulation (FTR).

The GSA announces the Fiscal Year federal *per diem* rates, which run from October 1 and run through the following September 30. Rates vary by city; to find the rates for each city go to **www.gsa.gov/perdiem**

IRS Optional Standard Mileage Reimbursement Rate

About 80% of all organizations use the IRS optional standard mileage reimbursement rate to compensate their employees who use their personal vehicles for company travel. The rate for the coming year is typically announced in November or December. Occasionally, if there is a large spike in oil prices the IRS will adjust the rate mid-year but this does not happen often.

Use of the rate is not mandatory. Some use a lower rate. We could find no one using a higher rate. If a higher rate were used it would trigger some income tax reporting issues for the organization and the employee receiving the payment. Check the IRS website for the current rate.

CHAPTER 11
CHECK AND CORPORATE CARD FRAUD: DETECTION AND PREVENTION

When it comes to any type of fraud, it is important to remember that it can come in two flavors: internal and external. While this chapter focuses mostly on the steps any organization needs to take to guard itself against external attacks, it is important to remember to incorporate strong internal controls throughout the payment process. This will help protect against internal fraud. This chapter focuses on check and p-card fraud specifically.

In this chapter we investigate:

- Check Fraud Issues
- Use of various types of positive pay
- Practices that enable internal check fraud
- P-card fraud issues
- Ways to minimize p-card fraud losses
- A 20 Step Plan to prevent p-card fraud

Check Fraud

Although check fraud has been with us for a long time, it continues to flourish. While much attention is given to new types of electronic payment fraud, and for good reason, it is important not to get complacent when it comes to the older more established check fraud.

The reason for this is simple. Check fraud remains the type of fraud that is most frequently attempted by crooks. So, any organization that lets down its guard on this front is apt to find itself with losses.

Common Methods Used to Commit Check Fraud

Most commonly, check fraud is committed using one of the following approaches;

>1. Forgery is used to place an unauthorized forged signature on the face of the check or to falsify the endorsement on the back before the check is deposited.

>2. Counterfeiting involves the creation of a check with information that was not intended. Various methods are used to either duplicate an existing check (with altered information) or to fabricate a new check using banking information that does not belong to the crooks.

>3. Alterations are not as common as they once were. This approach generally refers to the use of household chemicals and solvents to remove or modify handwriting and other information on a check.

While there are other approaches, these are the types readers are most likely to run into.

Who Is Responsible for the Losses?

While your gut instinct might be to say the bank would be responsible for any check fraud losses, since you clearly did not authorize a particular payment, this is not necessarily the case. At one time, banks did cover losses. However, the problem got so out of hand there were changes made to the Uniform Commercial Code (UCC) and that is no longer the case.

Today, losses are apportioned based on which party was in the best position to prevent the loss. This means every organization is supposed to exercise what is referred to as ordinary care in their check processes and incorporate reasonable commercial standards (which are not defined in the UCC).

That being said, common sense should play a key role in developing practices around the check production cycle.

When it comes to check stock, three safety features incorporated into the documents are considered the minimum. Some safety features include:

- Artificial Watermarks
- Chemical Reactive Paper
- Erasure Protection
- Invisible and Fluorescent Fibers.
- Laid Lines
- MICR Band
- MICR target alignment box
- Microprinting
- Non-Negotiable Stub Backer
- Padlock Security Icon
- Pantograph
- Rainbow Prismatic Colored Stock
- Sequential Numbering Security Feature Box
- Security Screen
- Simulated Watermark
- Void Pantograph
- Warning Box
- Watermark Certification Seal

Reasonable Care: Preprinted Check Stock

While most mid-size and large organizations have moved away from pre-printed check stock, there are still many organizations that use it. At a minimum, the check stock should be kept:

- Under lock and key
- With very limited access to check stock and
- Person who has key should not be the same person who prints checks, if possible.

Realize that banks do not check signatures on checks nor are they required to. Therefore, it is critical that proper care be taken of check stock.

Examples of Not Exercising Ordinary Care

Here are some examples of practices that would be considered NOT exercising ordinary care in the payment process:

- Not keeping pre-printed check stock locked in a secure location
- Not having appropriate segregation of duties
- Leaving a checkbook in an unlocked desk draw or filing cabinet, for Rush or emergency checks

Best Protection against Check Fraud: Positive Pay

Virtually every expert will tell you that using positive pay is simply the best safeguard your company has against check fraud. But be aware that this protection does not apply to other types of payment fraud. You need to take other steps in those arenas. The discussion below provides an explanation of positive pay and the enhancements some banks have introduced to make the product stronger.

Check fraud is a fact of business life. No matter how careful an organization is, it happens. Virtually every company gets hit at one point or another. By knowing what the risks and alternatives are you will be in the best position to limit your firm's exposure in case of check fraud.

Positive Pay and Its Cousins

While every check expert agrees positive pay is helps thwart check fraud, it has taken a lot of scrutiny on all fronts. Crooks are a resourceful lot and just as quickly as the legitimate business world develops protection against them, the fraudsters find ways to circumvent the safeguards. This has happened to some extent with positive pay and has led to some very interesting innovations as the corporate world protects itself against check fraud.

The Basic Model: The basic positive pay model requires that a company send a file to the bank each time it does a check run.

The file contains check numbers and dollar amounts of all checks issued. The bank then matches all checks that come in for clearing against this file. Once a check comes in and is paid, the item is removed from the file and cannot be paid again.

This approach took a big whack at the check fraud problem. It eliminated several huge check fraud issues including:

- The copying of one check numerous times and the subsequent cashing of all of them;

- The altering of the dollar amount on a check ; and

- The complete manufacture of fraudulent checks drawn on an organization's bank account.

What the basic model did not address were checks cashed by tellers and checks where the payee's name was changed. Additionally, companies that could not produce a check-issued file for transmission to their banks were left unprotected.

Other types of positive pay include:

- **Reverse Positive Pay:** Recognizing that not every organization was able or willing to produce the tape needed for positive pay, banks introduced another service. It's called reverse because it reverses the process. Each morning the bank tells the company what checks have been presented for clearing. It is up to the company to check those listings and make sure that they are all legitimate. Typically, there is a fall-back position if the company does not notify the bank and usually that is that the bank pays on the check. The action should be discussed with the bank when the reverse positive pay relationship is initially set up.

- **Payee Name Positive Pay**: Recognizing that fraudsters were reduced to focusing their efforts on changing the payee names on checks, a few banks have taken up the fight in that regard. In addition to the check number and dollar amount, they will also verify the payee name.

Will this completely stop check fraud? Probably not, but it certainly will make it more difficult for the crooks trying to separate your company from its funds.

Warning: Not Using Positive Pay??

If your organization is not using positive pay, ask to see the deposit agreement to make sure that bank has not passed the liability to your organization. Claiming ignorance will get you nowhere if a fraudulent check makes it through the system. Even if there is nothing in the deposit agreement, you might inquire from the treasurer, controller or whomever is responsible for banking relationships if the firm ever signed a letter refusing to accept positive pay.

Some banks require this and use it as a defense to shift payment responsibility to their customers in cases of check fraud. We've heard of several cases where the bank refused an account if positive pay wasn't used without a signed letter.

Practices that Enable Internal Check Fraud

Did you know that certain sloppy practices, especially when it comes to checks, actually make it easier for employees to commit check fraud? Allowing these practices to continue is effectively enabling the fraudsters who might be lurking in your corridors. And these are all things you can change without spending a cent. So what are these easy-to-fix processes?

- **Practice #1** Allowing checks to be returned to the person who requested them. Without a doubt, this is the biggest enabler of them all. And, sadly, it is a practice permitted in many, many organizations. While we concede there are rare occasions when the checks do need to be returned, they are few and far between. We recommend that any organization allowing it develop a form to be included with the check. The form should be filled out by the person requesting the return and a very senior executive should sign it. It should contain a place for the person to enter the reason the check must be returned and not mailed. The form works in two ways to deter fraud. First, few employees will want to get it signed unless the check really must be returned. And, second, a crook will think twice (hopefully) about documenting the request if he or she intends to steal the check.

- **Practice #2** Permitting rush or ASAP checks in all but the most urgent circumstances. When the data is analyzed, rush checks represent a disproportionate share of both fraudulent checks and duplicate payments. The reason is simple. Crooked vendors know if they call an organization's accounts payable department and threaten to put the company on credit hold, the chance of a rush manual check being issued is high. So that is exactly what they do. Even if the call is legitimate, the chances are a second or third invoice has been issued before the vendor got desperate enough to call and demand a rush check. Inevitably, the original invoice eventually makes its way into accounts payable and sometimes gets paid. Part of the reason for this is that the manual process sometimes results in records not being updated or entered correctly.

- **Practice #3** Lack of appropriate segregation of duties. Whenever one employee is authorized to perform two tasks that serve as checks and balances to each other, it increases the risk of fraud. So, making someone a check signer and giving them access to check stock or the ability to approve an invoice increases the ease with which they could commit check fraud, should they so desire. Therefore, especially when it comes to an organization's money, appropriate segregation of duties is crucial.

- **Practice #4** Giving high-level executives access to everything. In some ways, this is a subset of the issue discussed above. There are organizations that go out of their way to set up the appropriate segregation of duties and then give either a high-level executive or the accounts payable manager access to everything. This completely negates all other blocks. When questioned about it, inevitably the response is that the person in question is a trusted employee. Well, guess who commits most internal fraud? Long-term trusted employees!

- **Practice #5** Making all high-level executives authorized signers. In some organizations all vice presidents are put on bank accounts as signers, even if they never sign and check signing is not part of their job. As in the discussion above, this can negates the segregation of duties the organization strove to set up.

- **Practice #6** Poor master vendor file practices. So many organizations ignore their master vendor file not realizing they are providing the perfect hiding place for employees looking for ways to defraud them. This is especially true when the file is never cleansed and vendors not used in over 12 or 14 months are not deactivated. It is easy to put this task off when other issues are pressing. But don't; you are only asking for trouble by leaving inactive vendors in the file. Use of strict coding standards also helps. When was the last time your master vendor file was cleansed?

As we said at the beginning, these practices are fixable at virtually every organization—and the fix doesn't cost a red cent.

P-card Fraud

Fear of unauthorized use of a corporate credit card keeps many organizations from instituting a card program. This is truly unfortunate as card programs make the accounts payable function a lot more efficient and p-card fraud is one of the easiest to control. If you set up and monitor the program correctly, losses should be minimal.

Types of P-card Fraud

The unauthorized use of a company credit card can occur in one of several ways. They include:

- Use of organization's card to purchase goods for personal use
- Use of organization's card to purchase goods from a compliant vendor at an exaggerated price
- Taking kickbacks from vendor
- Use by a third-party, completely unrelated to the organization

Simple Approach to Limit P-card Fraud Losses

As noted in the introduction to this section, losses due to unauthorized use of a p-card can be severely limited. This can be done by:

- Setting very low daily and monthly limits, if that is all that is needed by the cardholder
- Set Merchant Category Code (MCC) restrictions
- If appropriate, set seasonal limits
- Only give cards to those who need them

By setting limits in concert with what the cardholder needs to do his or her job, the risk is lowered. If someone only charges $10 and $20 items several times a week, there is no reason for them to have a card with a $10,000 limit.

Likewise, many organizations block certain MCC codes such as casinos, jewelry stores and liquor stops.

A 20-Step P-card Fraud Prevention Plan

One issue that prevents some organizations from using p-cards is a fear of fraud. At AP Now we feel this is a real crime given the real benefits of a p-card program. We also strongly believe that a well-designed program administered correctly minimizes losses. What's more, the gross amount of payment card and third-party network transactions will be recorded on a new IRS form, form 1099-K – by the card issuer.

This little detail might finally push those on the fence into getting a p-card program. If the card issuer is reporting the payment on a 1099, the organization won't have to handle that reporting anymore. Consider switching those vendors who refuse to provide a W-9 to p-cards, if possible.

All-in-all, a well-designed p-card program is your first defense against fraud. What follows is a 20 step plan any organization can use to establish a best practice fraud-resistant p-card program. As you read through this you'll notice that most of the provisions will also apply to a Travel expense card program.

• **Step 1:** Create a written, detailed policies and procedures manual.

• **Step 2:** Update your policies and procedures regularly to reflect the p-card program roles and responsibilities accurately.

• **Step 3:** Share the written policy with everyone who may have anything to do with the program.

• **Step 4:** Make sure there are meaningful consequences for misuse of the p-card. This information should be shared with everyone who has a card and should be enforced.

• **Step 5:** Appoint a permanent p-card administrator with responsibility for the p-card program. If the program isn't large enough for a full-time administrator, give primary responsibility to someone who handles this chore along with other tasks.

• **Step 6:** Create a detailed cardholder agreement including wording that gives the organization the right to terminate the employee if the card is abused.

• **Step 7:** Require the signature of the cardholder and the cardholder's supervisor on the cardholder agreement before the employee is given his or her card.

• **Step 8:** Assign and communicate detailed roles and responsibilities for the transaction reconcilers and approvers.

• **Step 9:** If possible, use a p-card design that minimizes the possibility of "accidental" use. If the card looks like any other credit card, the odds of an employee pulling out the wrong card increase exponentially. But, if the card is bright purple or some other non-traditional color, the employee is less likely to mistakenly use the card.

• **Step 10:** Establish card limits that reflect the needs of the cardholder not his or her position. This reduces the chances of excessive or inappropriate use issues. These limits can be related to dollar amounts as well as MCC (merchant category code) restrictions.

• **Step 11:** Insist that all cardholders have some training before issuing a p-card to a new cardholder. Depending on the circumstances the training can be live or online.

• **Step 12:** Require refresher training periodically for continuing cardholders. This training should also be mandated for those who misuse the card. Again, the training can be live or online.

• **Step 13:** Require original receipts for every p-card purchase made. These should be submitted and spot checked. This is especially important if you don't get Level three data.

• **Step 14:** Require electronic transfer of cumulative data from the card-services provider for data mining and analysis based on known risk factors.

• **Step 15:** Wherever available, get Level 3 data and review it regularly. Letting cardholders know you will be receiving detailed information about all purchases serves as a strong deterrent to those contemplating p-card fraud.

• **Step 16:** Make sure to include p-cards in your hotline process where suspected abuse and fraud can be reported. Providing a confidential way for individuals to report suspected p-card fraud and abuse as well as publicizing that process will strengthen a p-card program exponentially.

• **Step 17**: Include an audit processes as part of the program to regularly evaluate compliance with program policies and requirements.

• **Step 18:** Make surprise audits an integral part of the program. This should include a unit's p-card documentation that disclosed irregularities in the explanations for nonstandard transactions and documentation.

• **Step 19:** Decide where you want the card used and then insist that employees follow those instructions. Do not permit the use of personal cards or having the organization invoiced if a p-card was the designated payment vehicle.

- **Step 20**: Continue to look for vendors who will accept your p-cards as well as expanded applications.

P-cards are a priceless tool for organizations looking to run an efficient payment function. Don't let a sloppily designed or implemented program ruin what could otherwise be a fine addition to your arsenal of payment tools. By following the 20 steps discussed above you will be well on your way to having a first class p-card program.

CHAPTER 12
ELECTRONIC PAYMENT FRAUD PREVENTION AND DETECTION

Electronic payment fraud is nasty, insidious and strikes at those who are least prepared. That's part of the reason most fraud experts recommend that professionals stay current on new and emerging payment frauds and techniques to stop them. This is a constantly evolving issue.

Complicating the issue is the fact that some of the crooks involved in this arena are very smart and continually find ways to create new frauds. This means constant vigilance on the part of the professionals charged with protecting their organization against any type of payment fraud.

In this section we investigate:

- Misconceptions that keep organizations from adequately protecting themselves against electronic payment fraud

- Electronic payment (ACH) Fraud

- Wire Transfer Fraud

- The emerging BYOD Issue and how it impacts every organization

Electronic Payment Misconceptions

When it comes to electronic payments, there are a few misunderstandings about the process that can (and have) cost organizations thousands, if not millions, of dollars. Let's take a look at five of those issues and see why they can cause problems.

- **Issue #1**. The belief that positive pay will protect the organization. Positive pay protects against check fraud; that is all. It does nothing to deter fraud in the electronic payment arena. In fact, the first form of electronic payment fraud was the re-presentment by crooks of transactions that had been bounced by positive pay. They simply presented the transactions the second time around as ACH debits, and the transactions flew through.

- **Issue #2**. The belief that those not making electronic payments are not at risk for this type of fraud. Unfortunately, this too is not correct. Everyone is at risk for electronic payment fraud. That's why every organization must take steps to protect itself.

- **Issue #3.** The belief that the bank will eat any losses for unauthorized payments. While this may have been true twenty-five years ago, it is no longer true. Changes to the UCC now make everyone responsible for exercising reasonable care. This is why it is imperative that all organizations figure out what needs to be done to protect the organization against fraud and then take the steps to implement those actions.

- **Issue #4.** The belief that the organization is so big, no crook would dare to steal from them. Again, this is false. A large organization might present a challenge to crooks, but one they are more than happy to take on given the potential pay out, if they are successful. Being large is no protection from fraudsters.

- **Issue #5.** The belief that the organization is too small, so no crook would bother to steal from them, given the small potential payout. Again, this is not true. Crooks know that some smaller organizations have weak controls making them easy targets. In fact, several years ago, a group of fraudsters went after a number of school districts in late August and between Christmas and New Year's Day. They picked these times because they knew the school districts were lightly staffed at these times. These particular thefts demonstrate not only the crooks willingness to go after smaller organizations but the level of preparation they undertake when picking targets.

Electronic Payment (ACH) Fraud

ACH fraud, sometimes referred to as electronic payment fraud, is a threat every organization must deal with on a daily basis. For no organization is exempt from the prying grasps of fraudsters trying to get into any bank account they can. Making this issue even more serious than readers might be aware is the fact that some of these thefts are being masterminded by organized crime located in other countries.

Do not be lulled into a false sense of security thinking that your organization is not a target. Neither non-participation in the market nor size of your organization will safeguard your accounts. Only you can do that by taking the necessary steps as discussed further in this piece. But before we get to the strategies you can use to protect your organization, we have a quick review of the growth of this type of fraud and a very brief description of the types of ACH fraud now in play.

Growth in ACH Fraud

The accompanying table shown on the bottom of this page shows the incidence of actual and attempted ACH fraud in the last three years. The numbers come from surveys done by the Association of Financial Professionals. Not all the frauds detailed in the survey were successful. In fact many weren't.

The numbers shown are broken into those actual and attempted frauds that were committed using ACH debits and ACH credits. Frauds relying on ACH credits are mainly account takeovers. As you can see, growth in that activity (both actual and attempted) has increased 100% in two years. Clearly, this is an area of concern.

The 24-Hour Rule

When it comes to uncovering unauthorized ACH transactions, time is really of the essence. While individuals have 60 days to uncover an unauthorized transaction and have the funds returned, everyone else has 24 hours. By everyone else, we mean anyone who isn't an individual person. This includes not-for-profits, municipalities, colleges, universities, cities etc.

If you uncover a fraudulent transaction after the 24 hour limit, don't feel all is lost. Still notify your bank immediately. While they may not be able to recover all your money, they may be able to get some of it back. This is one area where you simply cannot take your time investigating potential losses. Action must be taken quickly if you are to recover any of your money.

Types of ACH Fraud

The evolution of ACH fraud has been quite rapid. Just a few short years ago, the banking community was primarily concerned about the first type of fraud. Now, that has expanded.

Today, ACH fraud can be broken into six general types as follows:

- Representing positive pay rejects as ACH debits (unauthorized ACH debits)

- Account hijacking also called corporate account takeover (typically via the initiation of ACH credits)

- Reverse phishing – redirecting of electronic payments from a legitimate vendor to the fraudster

- e-Check payments to a third party using your bank account information

- Falsified e-mails coming from legitimate organizations containing either an attachment or a link to an illicit website. This is an alternate approach to getting information needed for an account hijacking.

- Man-in-the-e-mail scheme is an e-mail variation of a known man-in-the-middle scam. Fraudsters intercept legitimate e-mails between the purchasing and supply companies and then spoof subsequent e-mails impersonating each company to the other. The fraudulent e-mails directed the purchasing companies to send payments to a new bank account because of a purported audit. The bank accounts, of course, belong to the fraudsters, not the supply companies.

There will be others as the crooks in this arena are very smart. They understand how the technology works, how the banking system operates and take advantage of this knowledge for their own benefit—at your expense.

Prevention

While you can't stop someone from trying to steal from your organization, you can make it so difficult they are not successful. What follows is a list of tactics any organization can use to prevent a fraudster from winning when trying to steal from your firm using the ACH.

- Set up a separate computer for online banking activity only.

- Put ACH blocks on all accounts where ACH activity is not to be initiated; if you are paying using ACH credits, put ACH debit blocks on your accounts.

- Put ACH filters on accounts where ACH debit activity is permitted.

- Set up a single account for incoming wire transfers, allowing no other activity in that account. Sweep it each night into another account. This prevents someone who gets wire transfer information from using it to initiate unauthorized ACH debits.

- Establish other communication channels, such as telephone calls, to verify significant transactions. Arrange this second-factor authentication early in the relationship and outside the e-mail environment to avoid interception by a hacker. Do not give wire transfer information over the phone.

- Do not use the "Reply" option to respond to any business e-mails. Instead, use the "Forward" option and either type in the correct e-mail address or select it from the e-mail address book to ensure the real e-mail address is used.

- Issue refund checks from a separate account with a low-dollar limit.

- Regularly update of security and anti-virus software.

Detection

Sometimes, no matter how hard you try, an unauthorized transaction gets through. If that happens, all is not lost. If you notify the bank within 24 hours, they can retrieve your money. The following strategies are recommended for detecting unauthorized activity.

1) Perform daily bank reconciliations to identify unauthorized activity.

2) Notify the bank immediately of unauthorized activity.

Beware of sudden changes in business practices. For example, if suddenly asked to contact a representative at their personal e-mail address when all previous official correspondence has been on a company e-mail, verify via other channels that you are still communicating with your legitimate business partner.

Occasionally employees will use their personal e-mail addresses for company business, usually because the organization's firewall makes it difficult for certain messages to get through. Discourage this practice wherever possible. This is a particularly insidious type of fraud and every organization is a potential target.

Not only is it important that you update your procedures and protections now, but it is critical you keep on top of this issue as crooks are continually identifying new ways to get at your account.

Wire Transfer Fraud

In an era where alternative payment methodologies can be had for a tiny fraction of the cost of a wire transfer, this mechanism is losing a lot of its appeal, especially on the domestic front.

Since more wire transfers are handled outside of accounts payable, it is critical that all parties making transfers be aware of the potential for fraud. It is also important that they take the appropriate steps to ensure that they follow the same rules for making payments as are used when making other types of payments. If they don't, controls are weakened and the possibility for fraud and/or duplicate payments increases.

Wire Transfer Information Requests

This is an old problem that has persisted for many years. One of the pieces of information a crook needs to defraud your organization is your bank account number. This is especially true if the thief intends to produce phony checks. There are a number of ways to obtain this information but the easiest is to call up and ask for it. Clearly, if the crook calls and asks outright for the account number, they won't get the information they want.

Instead, they call up and say they are making a wire transfer to the company and ask for the wire instructions. Of course, when it looks like money is coming to the company; most employees willingly provide the information. That's part of the reason many companies don't make payments from the account that receives wire transfers. Funds from that account are swept each night into a general account.

Do not give wire information to anyone who calls on the phone or e-mails asking for it claiming they want to send your organization some money. Now if you are wondering what would happen if this were a legitimate request, you are not alone. Many organizations will provide this but only to someone they already know at the company using a phone number, e-mail address or fax number they already have on hand. Another words, the information is never given on the initial phone call. Otherwise, they could be inadvertently giving information that would help the fraudster.

Wire Transfer Fraud Prevention

There are a number of steps any organization making wire transfers can take to minimize the risk for a fraudulent transaction. They include:

- Set up a single account for incoming wire transfers, allowing no other activity in that account. Sweep it each night into another account.

- Never give wire transfer information over the phone, no matter who the person on the other end of the phone says they are.

- Set up a separate account for wires if you make them on a regular basis. If someone tries to write a check or initiate an ACH transaction against the wire transfer account, it will bounce.

- When making wire transfers by phone, take special care. This should only be done in cases of emergency as it is a weak process from a control standpoint. Before the wire it released the bank will call back a second individual at the company to verify the information. The person authorized to verify has been pre-established by the company and the names provided to the bank in advance. Basically, this process relies on voice recognition, which is not great. This control gets even weaker when the party who is the primary contact is out and the backup verifier provides the authorization.

- Always be alert for anything that looks odd. Better to ask questions beforehand than try and retrieve money after the fact.

The BYOD Issue

BYOD stands for Bring Your Own Device, and in this context, device refers to smartphone or tablet. Some include laptops in that definition. When Apple introduced the ipad in April 2010, not many saw it having anything to do with accounts payable in the foreseeable future. We've come a long way in a very short period of time.

It is estimated that 250 million tablets were sold in 2013. And it seems that there is continual news of new types of devices being introduced almost daily – okay, that's a slight exaggeration, but you get what I mean.

In the past, virtually all hardware used by professionals in the course of their jobs was purchased by their employers. This gave the company control over security issues and, to some limited extent; control over what their employees did with that hardware.

With the introduction of affordable tablets and smartphones that is changing. Individuals are purchasing these devices in droves for their personal use and then utilizing them for work purposes as well. This makes them more productive and gives them greater flexibility.

The use of personal devices for business purposes has been going on for a few years now. The first reports we had were of managers using their smartphones during business meetings to release (or approve) wire transfers and ACH transactions. The device gave them the ability to multi-task. So, what's the problem, you ask?

The Security Issue

Most organizations take the security of the computers used by their employees very seriously. Anti-fraud and virus protection software is loaded onto the machines and updated regularly. What's more, many organizations have guidelines for their staff as to how and when different programs can be used. And many organizations block some or all of the social media sites (like Facebook, LinkedIn and YouTube).

All this goes out the door when employees use their own personal devices for company business. Even if virus protection software was originally put on the device, many people don't regularly update it. Most regularly surf the Internet with their devices. And, some visit websites that might be prone to enabling malware attacks. All this flies in the face of what best-practice organizations have been doing to protect their technology and information from invasions from fraudsters.

Now, to be fair, virtually all employees who bring their own devices to work to use for business, think they are doing a good thing. They are certainly not looking to weaken the organization's defenses against fraudsters. This is such a new issue; the implications have not been analyzed or discussed much. And many employees are not aware there are issues.

The Corporate Stance

There are two basic ways to address this issue. To begin with, every organization needs to analyze the issue and have a corporate policy. Right now, only about one-quarter of all organizations have a policy (and we suspect most of those organizations are larger ones.).

The policy can take one of two thrusts:

- **Employees are asked not to use their personal devices for company business.** In this case, the policy is mandatory and employees are not given any leeway.

- **Employees are permitted to use personal devices, but only after they bring them to IT and have the appropriate anti-virus software loaded onto the machine.** They are also required to bring the devices back periodically to have the software updated.

Unfortunately, at this point, most organizations are silent on this issue. This is an issue that needs to be brought to management's attention. At that point, a task force comprised of IT folks and all interested/affected business users can make a recommendation on what the organization's BYOD policy should be.

Accounts payable should fight to be part of this task force. This is a critical issue for the accounts payable function. While many of the other business users on this task force will be concerned about their data integrity (and this is an important issue, not to be disparaged) accounts payable is concerned about a critical issue: the organization's money, its lifeblood.

The Future for BYOD

Clearly, these devices are not going away. If anything, they will become more prevalent as new uses are found for them. What's more, some are predicting a change in the way some companies handle the purchase of IT for their employees.

Of course, many will stay the current course of providing employees with the hardware or devices they select. That presents problems for some employees who could conceivably end up carrying around two cell phones and two tablets. Such a scenario would not make their lives any easier.

Some see a move towards companies giving employees an "allowance" if they prefer to purchase their own devices rather than rely on those provided by the organization. For example, a company might give an employee who had a business need for a tablet and a smartphone, a $600 annual stipend toward the purchase of these devices and perhaps a $50 monthly allowance towards monthly charges. Employees who took this option would be on their own in the case of upgrades or problems. Employees who went with the company-recommended devices could rely on IT for help in case of upgrades or problems.

There is no simple answer to what's the best policy when it comes to BYOD. This is a new and evolving issue and it will take some time to sort all the issues out. What's more, as you can probably guess, there will be additional issue to address. You might even have thought of some of them while reading this piece.

Developing Related Issues

Clearly the first concern for any organization is developing a policy that addresses all the issues and concerns generated by this new technology. Additionally, other issues related to BYOD include:

- **Issue #1** Are there any tax reporting consequences for providing devices and allowances to employees?

- **Issue #2** If the employee purchases a device with a company "allowance" who owns the device? Does this ownership change over time? Does it matter if the company only paid for part of the device and not the whole thing?

- **Issue #3** If the organization provides a stipend towards the purchase of a device, how long is the employee expected to use that device before purchasing a new one?

- **Issue #4** If the employee leaves the organization, who owns the device purchased with a company allowance? Does it matter who initiated the separation? Is there a difference in policy depending on whether the employee left of his/her own volition and the employee who was laid off or fired? What if the person in question was fired for an egregious cause?

- **Issue #5** If the employee leaves, what happens to company data on a device purchased by an employee, without any financial help from the organization?

CHAPTER 13
OTHER TYPES OF FRAUD AFFECTING THE ACCOUNTS PAYABLE FUNCTION

In addition to the straightforward types of fraud affecting the accounts payable process, there are other types of fraud impacting an organization's payment process. In this section we take a look at a few of them including:

- Employee Fraud
- Expense reimbursement Fraud
- Billing Fraud
- Check Request Fraud

Fraud comes in two flavors: internal and external. While no one likes to think about it, virtually every organization is vulnerable for both. There is a side benefit from installing best practices to deter fraud, and it is a big one. Many of the strategies and tactics used to deter crime will also deter duplicate payments. So by instituting fraud-deterrent practices, you will at the same time be improving your accounts payable operations, and taking a whack at the duplicate payment issue, which virtually every organization has.

Internal Fraud

While no one likes to acknowledge that one of their employees might steal from them, it is a fact of life. An organization's greatest vulnerability is not from the new employee, the one who is given little access, but rather from the long-term, trusted employee. This is, unfortunately, who commits the lion's share of insider fraud and the losses associated with their frauds tend to be higher.

A favored technique for those committing internal fraud—either by himself or herself or in collusion with the vendor—is allowing checks to be returned to requistioners. Lesson: don't allow it.

External Fraud

Vendors are not all honest and, in fact, some of them are downright dishonest. And some, while not dishonest, tend to be sloppy when it comes to preparing your invoices. So using the practices we advocate here will help you find errors made by your vendors, regardless of whether they were trying to defraud you or just made a mistake.

Phony vendors abound with schemes that have been going on literally for decades. Apparently they still work. You may get invoices for copier supplies, yellow pages ads, help wanted ads that you did not order etc., etc. Be vigilant requiring a completed PO for everything ordered. Good master vendor file practices will also help in this regard.

Be wary of vendors screaming for payment. Most crooks know that if they threaten credit holds, accounts payable will issue a rush check.

Always do some sort of checking to make sure new vendors are legitimate. This should be done before the vendor is entered into the master vendor file and that first payment is made.

Other basic best practices that make fraud more difficult include:

- Have the appropriate segregation of duties for all processes for everyone in the company—no exceptions.
- Use strong internal controls across all functions.

146

- Allow surprise audits—especially if you still have a petty cash box.

- Run your employees address file from HR against the addresses in the master vendor file. Check any matches closely.

- Do your bank reconciliations in a timely manner.

- If at all possible, install an anonymous tip hotline.

Fraud *will* happen. It's your job to make it so difficult to commit it against your organization that crooks turn their attention elsewhere.

An Ugly Issue: Employee Fraud Prevention

No one likes to admit it but occasionally an employee will steal from their employer. What's even more disheartening is that year after year, the statistics demonstrate that the most likely people to steal from their employers are long term trusted employees. Now before a few of our readers are offended by that allegation, let me point out that the thieves among us are few and far between. The problem is identifying the crook is not easy. They look like every other long term trusted employee. Let's take a look at some tactics every organization should employ to avoid an employee-theft disaster.

The Big Problem

The reason that organizations with strong internal controls are at such high risk is simple. Their employees know where the weaknesses are and know how to exploit them. What's more, some organizations have great segregation of duties controls set up and then they negate the whole thing by giving one or two "trusted employees" access to everything. Often this works fine, but occasionally it does not.

The other misconception that makes it easy for in-house fraudsters is the sense of complacency some organizations have. They think "it would never happen here" or "we're too big or too small." More than one executive has had to eat his or her our-employees-would-never-steal-from-us words.

Overriding Fraud Prevention/Detection Guidelines

Ideally, your goal should be to deter all potential frauds. By this I mean the controls and monitoring you have in place are so stringent that no one even attempts to steal from your organization. The only problem is there is no way to measure frauds that were deterred so you never really know if you were effective on this front.

If you haven't deterred a fraud and someone is bold enough to try, your next goal should be to prevent it. By this we mean, catch the fraud before the money leaves your bank account. And, finally, if the money does get away, you want to have processes in place to identify the fraud and hopefully recover the funds. If you can't recover the funds, at least you can put a stop to the fraud, if it is ongoing. Many employee frauds are continuing.

The following three principal guidelines will help you structure a framework that will serve to both deter and prevent fraud in your organization.

- Establish a strong internal control framework covering all facets of the payment function. This includes purchasing and receiving and of course, travel and entertainment reimbursements.

- Take segregation of duties seriously and make sure one person cannot do more than one part of the purchase-to-pay process. Regularly review the scope of your employees' access to ensure nothing has gone awry.

- Create a Policy of Zero Tolerance when it comes to any type of fraud or abuse. The policy should come from the highest level executive in the organization along with a letter stating the organization intends to abide by it across all spectrums.

What Else

There are a number of other tactics savvy organizations use, although you'd be amazed to discover the number of businesses that ignore these principles. What follows is a look at three simple steps any organization can use to both prevent and detect fraud.

1) **Mandatory vacations.** Anyone associated with any part of the payment function should be required to take five consecutive days off and someone else should perform their job function. The theory behind this approach is that in five days an ongoing fraud will unravel. Too often we hear staffers complain that their organization won't allow them to take their vacation because everyone is overworked. This is just asking for trouble. Not only has the organization ignored the five-consecutive vacation tactic, there's a good chance they have an unhappy employee.

2) **Job Rotation.** This strategy is a little harder to implement if you have a smaller department. And, to be blunt, there are certain functions that cannot be rotated. Asking the corporate head of tax to switch positions with the company's top lawyer is just not going to work. However, if you have more than three or four processors, rotating the suppliers they cover every six months or a year is very feasible. This makes collusion more difficult. What's more, you get the added benefit of having more than one person knowledgeable about different accounts. If you do take this step, and we recommend that you do, it is imperative that you have a strict coding standard and the associates handling your invoices all process exactly the same.

3) **Surprise Audits.** First and foremost, we're talking about surprise audits of the petty cash box, if you still have one. As regular readers know, we recommend the elimination of the petty cash box as a best practice. But, assuming you have one, surprise audits are one way to detect and prevent games in that arena. But, that is not the only auditing you should be doing. Periodically, audit your processors to ensure they are sticking to your rigid guidelines for handling invoices.

The Role of Expense Reimbursement Fraud

When it comes to travel and entertainment (expense reimbursement) fraud, many people think it is much ado about nothing. Since the dollars involved are typically small compared to other frauds, they argue, why not just ignore it. There are several very good reasons why even small dollar fraud should be dealt with.

> 1)   Fraud is fraud and if you want to run a strong ethical company no amount of fraud should be tolerated.
>
> 2)   Crooks tend to get bolder with every successful episode. So, what starts out as a $20 fraud will escalate with each business trip. Readers should note that on average, T&E frauds go on for two years.
>
> 3)   Many larger frauds are discovered because the thief could not resist dipping into the T&E pot. When an investigation of the faulty expense reimbursement requests were initiated, the larger frauds were uncovered. So, even if the first two reasons haven't convinced you to be vigilant about expense reimbursement fraud, this last item should get everyone's attention.

If You Suspect Fraud

The first thing to remember if you suspect fraud is that you could be wrong. Not everything is as it appears. So, before accusing do a little research and gather your facts. For, if you accuse some and you are wrong, you will never have the trust of that person again. What's more; the organization's relationship with that person will be strained for some time.

The second reason you don't want to accuse someone before you have all the facts is that you may alert them giving them time to either destroy needed evidence or flee. So, if you don't accuse the person, what should you do?

Tactics to Stop Travel & Entertainment Expense Shenanigans

The games employees play with their expense reimbursement expense requests are endless, giving new meaning to the phrase, "life is stranger than fiction." Typically, when we talk about shenanigans in the expense reimbursement realm, we mean deceitful reimbursement requests. These requests are typically, but not always, for smaller dollar amounts. Many people do not consider this fraud – but it is. Anytime someone fudges their records and requests reimbursement for funds not spent on authorized company business it's fraud – whether the money involved is one dollar or one million dollars.

When it comes to setting up an expense reimbursement policy, organizations are encouraged to assume the worst and protect against it. While it is definitely true that most employees will not try to scam their employers, a few will. And a few others will not realize that what they are doing falls outside what most would consider reasonable. Every organization has a few employees severely lacking in common sense.

Often because the dollar amounts involved may not be that large, these issues are not taken seriously. But keep in mind that every dollar reimbursed incorrectly is a dollar that comes right off the bottom line for the organization. In times when everyone is scrutinizing every last cent spent, there's absolutely no reason to pay for items that are not covered by your travel and entertainment policy. What follows are five policies every organization should use to guard against expense reimbursement shenanigans.

Tactic #1 Have a detailed written policy travel and entertainment policy. It should spell out what is expected as well as what the organization will reimburse the employee for. If there are some items that will not be reimbursed, this should be spelled out as well. The most common of these is liquor, if the organization does not reimburse for it. This is an area where assuming your employees have common sense will cause problems. Don't leave anything up to their discretion. You will quickly find that you have one or more employees severely lacking in this arena.

Your policy will only protect the organization if you incorporate consequences for not adhering to the policy. If you don't your policy will not do the job you want it to do. And, the more employees are able to push items through that should not be reimbursed, the more this problem will grow as they share their "successes" with each other.

Tactic #2 Insist on use of a corporate card for all business travel. Without going through all the different smarmy games employees can play when they use personal credit cards, suffice it to say that by insisting on the corporate card, you stop those games before they have a chance to get off the ground.

If employees insist on using personal cards, even after being given a company card, take action. Warn them that the next time, they will not be reimbursed and then stick to your guns, if they use their personal card after receiving the warning.

Tactic #3 Require the detailed meal receipt as well as a receipt for every item where reimbursement is requested. Again, this eliminates many of the games employees play with their expense reports. The detailed meal receipt lets you monitor the liquor issue as well as how many people actually attended the meal. The receipt for every expenditure requirement eliminates the games that more than a few play requesting reimbursement just below the receipt level.

We should be clear that just because we recommend you collect all the receipts, we are not advocating you check every last receipt, unless you uncover a problem. Continue using the spot checking approach that you utilize for all receipts, including the meal receipts in your verification process.

Tactic #4 Make managers responsible for the expense reimbursement reports they approve. Too many of the expense reimbursement shenanigans and frauds occur because the employee knows from experience that his or her manager is not going to review the expense report. They've seen the manager take the report and sign on the approved line without ever looking at the report. They bank on this behavior to ensure their games will fly under the radar.

Just telling the manager that he or she should review the expense report before approving it is likely to make little impact or change this behavior. In order for that to happen there has to be consequences for the failure to review. While one or two organizations have gone so far as to incorporate firing for the manager as well as the employee as the consequence for failure to review should a completely inappropriate approved expenditure surface, most organizations are not willing to take this step for simply failing to review the expense report. However, including this as an item in the annual review, and perhaps reducing the annual increase of any manager found approving an expense report with items on it that were obviously inappropriate or fraudulent is a step some are willing to take.

Tactic #5 Enforce the travel and reimbursement policy uniformly. This relatively simple approach will save you much aggravation. However, getting management's backing may not be as easy as it sounds. In an AP Now survey of its readers, 80% reported uniform enforcement of their policy. Alas, this means 20% were not enforcing it uniformly across the board.

The problem with uneven enforcement of the policy is two-fold. First, there is the obvious financial loss due to the excessive expenditure approved for payment. This is money that comes right out of the organization's profit, dollar for dollar. But there is another issue, more insidious, that is often ignored. Uneven enforcement encourages other employees to emulate the behavior of those playing games. They think, "Well if so-and-so can put in for whatever, why can't I?"

What's more, these creative expense items tend to get larger over time. The Association of Certified Fraud Examiners report that most expense reimbursement frauds go on for two years. So, while each individual amount may not be large, the amounts attributable to items that should not have been included can add up.

A Strong Travel & Entertainment Policy Prevents Trouble

The loosey-goosey approach to Travel and Entertainment spending acceptable in some organizations in the past is fast becoming unacceptable. While the employees who benefited may have appreciated the philosophy, it was bad for employee morale and the bottom line. The first crack in the free-spending reimbursement policies was fired by the likes of Enron and WorldCom. Strike two came with the passage of Sarbanes-Oxley many organizations (both public and private) took a second look and reigned in their policy.

The economy was responsible for the third strike. Let's face it, most organizations need to conserve every last cent and wasteful entertainment expenditures have no place in that environment. Uncontrolled travel and entertainment spending has struck out. But that does not mean that the current practices will die easy should an organization decide to reign in free-wheeling spending.

Once the decision to tighten enforcement of the policy has been made, you need to take action. What follows is a nine step plan any organization can use to change its T&E policy to a more stringent one.

The Plan

> • Step 1: Update your T&E manual paying special attention to the details. Don't be vague. Spell out clearly what's allowed and what's not. If you leave anything to common sense you'll quickly find out that a few of your employees have very little sense when it comes to spending your organization's money.

> • Step 2: Share the manual with every employee who might need to have access to it. This includes the administrative staff who might fill out expense reports for your executives as well as the occasional traveler.

> • Step 3: Put a cover letter on your updated T&E manual and have it signed by the highest level executive willing to endorse and support the policy, ideally the CEO or the CFO.

> • Step 4: Your policy should include strong zero tolerance policy language, making it clear that the organization will not tolerate anything but complete adherence to the policy.

• Step 5: Demand that approvers actually review what they approve. This can be done by holding them responsible for policy abuse or misuse. While in most cases it is not reasonable to expect the manager to be financially responsible, failure to review expense reports before approving them, can and should be an issue at performance review time.

• Step 6: Enforce the policy uniformly so there can be no finger pointing and claims of unfairness. This includes high level executives and sales people.

• Step 7: Use a corporate travel or p-card for all travel expenditures. Make it a requirement. This prevents those few employees who are tempted to make a few extra dollars on airfare from going down that route. Enterprising employees committing this fraud book two tickets. They get the receipt from the expensive ticket, use the receipt for reimbursement purposes, and return the ticket for reimbursement. They then take the cheaper flight.

• Step 8: Demand reimbursement from any employee who makes an unauthorized expenditure using the corporate card.

• Step 9: Give processors the authority to question any item on any report. They should regularly inquire about a certain number of items, especially when you first go public with your new policy.

What Else

There are a few other tactics organizations with tight T&E policies use. For starters, no employee should be able to approve expenditures for any event where he or she was one of the guests. This means that the highest level person should pick up the bill. If this is not possible the T&E report should be forwarded to the next highest level person for approval. While many companies already have language to this effect in their policies, others don't. In fact, in some organizations it is a common tactic for the lower level person to pick up the tab at questionable functions, say regular Friday afternoon lunches with no real business purpose.

Additionally, some organizations are taking the step of having a second approver on all reports. This approach tends to make the first approver a little more conscientious. To be perfectly honest, we do not see this becoming a common practice. However, what we do see happening is organizations requiring a second approval on reports over a certain dollar level. The exact level will depend on the nature of your business. Some organizations with hefty international travel have set this limit at $10,000 with half of that being easily eaten up by airfare. Firms that adopt a second-signature-over-certain-dollar-amounts policy should expect to see a rise in the number of reports submitted as some employees attempt to avoid that second level of scrutiny by submitting multiple expense reports for lower amounts.

We haven't discussed automation yet. There are numerous wonderful products on the market today that streamline the process of checking for policy compliance and automate the approval and reimbursement process. Some are available on a very reasonable pay-as-you-go basis. Where it is possible to include an automated review, policy compliance is likely to improve.

We're in a whole new business world and T&E is no exception. Utilizing a program such as the one discussed above will make your program more effective.

Phony Billing Scheme Shenanigans

Phony billing schemes are particularly difficult to uncover when a high-level company executive is involved. This is especially true when he/she appears to be ordering goods and/or services that they normally would order as part of their jobs. This is precisely what is alleged to have happened recently at a large food company. Here's a look at what happened, and more importantly, some steps that might have prevented the problem in the first place.

The Fraud: A vice president (VP) from the company in question is accused of siphoning over $600,000 from the company's marketing budget to help pay for personal expenses, including the professional softball team he helped sponsor

How The Fraud Was Perpetrated: Over a period of three years, it is believed the VP submitted false vendor invoices to the company for amounts believed to exceed $600,000. These invoices, which company officials approved, were for items including branded promotional items (hats, tee-shirts etc.) as well as promotional activities including fishing and spring training trips.

In reality, according to those connected with the case, the vendors submitting the invoices were businesses owned by an associate of the VP. The associate shared the money with the VP in cash and also used the funds to pay for trips, hotel rooms, rental cars and other expenses related to a softball team, they both sponsored.

How It Was Detected: In this case, the company uncovered the potential fraud through internal oversight and audit. They also alerted authorities, which is rare.

How It Could Have Been Prevented: Any one of the following might have prevented the suspected fraud.

> • Good vendor set-up practices, including vendor verification at the beginning
>
> • Strict segregation of duties – if the VP ordered the goods/services, he/she shouldn't have been the person monitoring the receiving or the fact services had been completed.
>
> • Stricter oversight of the budget, including comparison to previous years' expenditures.
>
> • Requirement for multiple bids for all items, including marketing expenditures.

Other Phony Billing Schemes Deterrents: Most phony billing schemes do not have all the elements to make them look legitimate that this one did. Here are a few other signs to look for when investigating for fraudulent invoices.

> • Invoices for unspecified consulting services

- Invoices with details lacking as to the goods ordered

- Invoices for services that do not clearly spell out what those services are

- Vendors with company names consisting only of initials; While many such companies are legitimate, crooks commonly use this naming convention

- Vendor billings more than once a month, for services

- Vendor addresses that match employee addresses – this is an easy catch and every one should be verifying that no vendor address matches an employee address

- A large spike in purchases from one vendor.

- Large billings broken into multiple smaller invoices, each of which is for an amount just under the approval level

Without a doubt, this is a difficult fraud to catch and/or prevent. It involves a high-ranking employee who understood how the payment approval process worked. Invoices that could have been legitimate were used to perpetrate the fraud. What's more, it appears there was a willing accomplice at a legitimate outside company. However, proper controls and appropriate segregation of duties might have helped. And, in the end, internal audit came through.

How to Avoid Check Request Fraud and the Resulting Duplicate Payments

Ahhh...check requests, that ubiquitous form used to request payments for all sorts of things. Theoretically a solution (by making it easy to request a payment when an invoice is missing) in reality it can create numerous headaches for accounts payable, not to mention causing duplicate payments by the boatload. Here's a look at some of the problems surrounding check requests and a few suggestions on avoiding them.

FUNDAMENTALS of ACCOUNTS PAYABLE

Background

Check requests are used in most organizations to request payment when an invoice is not available or was never provided. Ideally, there should be backup documentation augmenting the check request and providing details regarding the payment amount, the payee, and the reason for the payment. Since most payments made on check request forms will *not* go through the rigorous three-way match in accounts payable, the documentation supporting the check request is of utmost importance.

The one exception to this is those organizations that require a check request for every single payment. This is not a best practice, although some organizations with unique industry or regulatory requirements might find it necessary to go this route.

Where Check Requests Cause Problems

Check requests forms are often used to accommodate rush check requests. These are one-time payments made to vendors outside the normal invoice submission process. Typically this happens when a payment is late and the upset vendor threatens to put the organization on credit hold.

Whether the check request form is used for a rush check or simply because the invoice has been misplaced if the proper documentation is not attached the chances for a duplicate payment skyrocket. Ideally the attached documentation should be the original invoice. Of course, if it were available, there might be no need for the check request form.

Without the invoice to perform the three-way match, the purchase order and receiver often remain open on the organization's books. This can blossom into two types of problems. The most obvious is a duplicate payment made when the invoice finally shows up and is paid in accounts payable.

The final problem relates to fraud. Alas, a great number of fraudulent payments, more than we'd like to think, are issued on check requests. How is this possible? The most obvious answer is a crooked employee fills out the check request form and either convinces an authorized signer to sign it or forges the signature himself.

The other way that fraud occurs with a check request form is in response to an irate vendor claiming non-payment. Some vendors have learned if they get on the phone and are generally abusive with the accounts payable staff threatening credit holds, they can sometimes get a harried controller to sign off on a check request form authorizing the payment.

In one of the most egregious examples of this type of fraud a vendor pulled this screaming stunt every month for 18 months—getting double payment for each one. With murky documentation attached to each form, it was difficult to find the duplicates until the entire vendor file was pulled and reviewed.

Recommended Check Request Practices

There are a number of steps any organization can take to make the check request form work as it is intended without introducing the problems discussed above. Begin by requiring documentation for every check request form. If an invoice, or copy of an invoice, is not available, attach a copy of the contract, an e-mail detailing requirements, or whatever is available. Great care should be taken to avoid sending in the form without any supporting documents

In the extreme cases where no documentation is available—and you know that will happen at some point—require an extra signature of a very high-level executive within the organization, perhaps the controller or the CFO. The person making the request should be ready with a *really* good explanation for why the check should be issued without documentation. Requests without documentation should be few and far between. If there are outstanding POs and receivers related to these requests, that information should be included on the form so accounts payable can extinguish them when the payment is made.

If by some miracle, there is an invoice attached to the check request form, perform the normal three-way match extinguishing both the purchase order and the open receiver.

Reducing the Number of Check Request Forms

If you only have a few check request forms each month to process, there is, in all likelihood, little you can do to decrease the number of them. Like rush checks, a small number is an inevitable part of doing business.

If you get more than a few, for several months, track the requests keeping a log noting:

- The requestor;
- The payee;
- The date of the request; and
- The reason for the request.

When you have the data for a few months, take it out and analyze it. Are most of your requests coming from a few requestors? In that case you might want to have some discussions with those involved to determine where the problem lies.

But before you do that, take a look at the vendors receiving the payments. Are a suspiciously high number of these requests going to the same vendor? This could mean one of two things. The less sinister explanation is that there is a problem somewhere in the process that needs to be fixed so the vendor can receive payment through the normal cycle. The more ominous reason is that there is an ongoing fraud.

If you suspect fraud, do not approach the individuals involved. Get all your facts lined up ask your immediate supervisor to review them and if you both agree something is fishy, get HR involved. They will know the correct way to approach this situation. Discretion is crucial in these cases for two reasons. First, you could be wrong and, secondly, if you are correct, you don't want to tip your hand before the experts decide how to approach the matter.

Check request forms are a necessary evil in the accounts payable world. Work hard to implement best practices surrounding them and the troubles they cause will be held to a minimum.

Reimbursing employees for legitimate business expenses as spelled out in the travel and entertainment policy is what accounts payable (or the travel and entertainment group) is supposed to do. That is their responsibility. The reason for their review is to uncover items that should not be reimbursed. By employing the tactics discussed above, you will be on the road to achieving that mission. What's more, you will not have to wonder whether the employee tried to mislead you on purpose or simply didn't know any better. The strategies discussed should help stop both shenanigans and fraud dead in their tracks.

CHAPTER 14
THE ACCOUNTS PAYABLE POLICY AND PROCEDURES MANUAL

Every accounts payable department should have a procedures manual, to serve not only as a guide in case of emergency, but also to provide managers with the necessary documentation to demonstrate to management the capabilities of the staff and the work they are handling. Without such a document, few understand the scope of information that is needed to run a successful department. This is especially important for those organizations subject to the strictures of the Sarbanes-Oxley Act.

In this chapter we'll go over:

- The rationale for having a manual

- A Process to keep it updated

- When the policy needs to be changed

- Multiple uses for the manual

- Alternatives for Those Who Don't Have A Policy and Procedures Manual

Overview

Many organizations now post their accounts payable policy and procedures manual on their company intranet sites. This makes the information available to anyone who needs it, makes updating it relatively easy, and keeps it on the forefront of everyone's mind. It also makes it easy to refer people with questions to the manual rather than have accounts payable answer every question. From a control standpoint, this is recommended.

It forces everyone to use the same source document for procedures rather than relying on one individual's memory, which may or may not be accurate. Readers should be aware that having a policy and procedures manual can come back to haunt them if the staff does not adhere to it. By posting it on the intranet, or making it readily available using some other mechanism, the department is announcing its requirements. It makes it relatively easy to uncover situations where the policy is not adhered to by the accounts payable staff.

The Rationale for a Policy & Procedures Manual

Policy and procedures manuals are important for several reasons. For starters, the manual documents exactly how your accounts payable operates. It should cover every little detail. This is critically important if you are following the recommended best practice of standardizing your procedures. Standardization is important if you want to minimize or perhaps even eliminate duplicate payments. If all your processors handle invoices in exactly the same manner, you will have taken a giant step towards eliminating duplicate payments.

Once you have a detailed accurate policy and procedures manual it will serve as a valuable training tool. Not only will new employees be able to utilize it as they learn the ropes, your existing employees will be able to refer to it any time they are not quite certain how to handle a particular issue. Most departments have certain tasks that are only performed a few times a year. A detailed updated policy and procedures manual will guide your staff on the right way to handle each of those jobs.

And finally, for our readers working for public companies, there are Sarbanes-Oxley considerations. Having a manual is one step towards demonstrating appropriate controls, assuming it has been updated recently.

A Process to Keep It Updated

Once the manual is completed, don't put it on the shelf and forget about it. For starters, it should be shared with all your processors and anyone else who might need access. Small portions of it should be published and widely disseminated. This will include portions like your check cut off dates and your yearend schedule. If you have an Intranet for company use only, the manual might be posted there.

Any time you change your processes, make sure to update the policy and procedures manual. This not only includes process improvements but also big technology changes. Updating the manual should be part of any big project. Finally, don't forget to periodically ask processors for recommendations for changes.

At least once a year, review the manual to make sure it still reflects the processes in use in the accounts payable department. In many cases small process changes are made and no one thinks to update the manual.

Finally, should a major change be made, especially one affecting other departments, consider issuing an update email reminding all those impacted by the changes of the ramifications. For example, if you change your cutoff times, you might want to alert everyone who sends invoices in for payment. These updates might go to your employees and in some instance they may also go to your vendors.

Your policy and procedures manual can serve as the backbone of any accounts payable department but only if it accurately reflects the work being done there. It is up to the manager to see that it is kept updated so it can do its job adequately.

Updating the Accounts Payable Policy & Procedures Manual

Policy and procedures manual have a lot in common with wills. We all know we should have one and should periodically update it, but few of us keep it updated once we *finally* get around to getting it done. Now, in light of Sarbanes-Oxley with its onerous documentation requirements, the manual is something every accounts payable department should have. Of course, most readers don't need an Act of Congress to make them aware that they should have a written manual. What follows is a simple step-by-step plan anyone can follow. While the theory is simple, we are the first to concede that executing it is not.

- **Step one**: Find your old policy and procedures manual and dust if off.

- **Alternative step one**: If you don't have an existing manual, or if the one you have is so out of date, it is hopeless, begin by making a list of all the topics to be covered. See our offer in the Help Getting Started section below for a tool to help you in that process.

- **Step two**: Review the manual and mark off all processes that have changed.

- **Step three**: Make a note of new processes that need to be added.

- **Step four**: Either assign one person to make all the changes or better yet, assign different sections to different staff members. Ideally the assignments should match their responsibilities.

- **Step five**: Set a deadline when the draft material is due back. Make sure everyone is aware of the deadline.

- **Step six**: A week before your deadline, send a reminder e-mail to everyone working on the project.

- **Step seven**: Two days before your deadline, send another reminder e-mail.

- **Step eight**: Collect all sections and review. If you disagree with anything written, discuss it with the author.

- **Step nine**: Have all changes reviewed. Do this by giving each section to someone other than the person who wrote it.

- **Step ten**: Resolve any discrepancies.

- **Step eleven**: Verify that what is written in the manual is actually how the work is being processed in your department.

- **Step twelve**: Publish and publicize. If at all possible, the manual should be put on your company Intranet site with access given to any employee who might need it. Highlight your check production and cut-off schedules.

- **Step thirteen**: Thank everyone who was involved.

- **Step fourteen**: Every six or twelve months, repeat the process.

When the Policy Needs to Be Changed

Whether it's your travel and entertainment policy, the way your p-cards are used or how you expect vendors to interact, getting people to change is not an easy task. They get set in their ways and don't want to change. And, let's face it; in all likelihood your change is not going to be something they are happy about. Employ the following five steps and your changes should be accepted with a little less complaining and shenanigans.

- **Step 1** *Have the change signed by someone with authority*. This ensures that no one will try and do an end run around the accounts payable department, getting approval to ignore the new policy from a higher level executive.

- If the change is likely to affect everyone in the company, having the new policy announced under the signature of the CFO or COO or even the CEO is a great way to ensure compliance. If the change is going to affect only the accounts payable staff, having the policy signed off on and announced by the accounts payable manager might do the trick in some cases and in others the controller might need to be the one whose signature goes on the new policy. Finally, if you are trying to make a change affecting your vendors, make sure you get purchasing on board. The announcement to the suppliers could be signed by a finance/accounting and procurement executive.

- **Step 2** *Spell out exactly what the new policy is.* Don't assume everyone knows what you mean. Inevitably there will be a few people who don't see things the way you think they should. So, don't give them any wiggle room.

- **Step 3** *Set an effective date.* Don't give them the chance to claim ignorance as to when the policy was to be implemented. Effective immediately might seem good enough, but it might not be enough. You might even mark the effective date the day before you send your announcement to fully avoid any games.

- **Step 4** *Spell out the consequences for not adhering to the policy.* If there are no repercussions for not complying, you'll have less than 100% compliance. For example, if you are announcing a policy of not paying for charges put on personal cards, say "we will no longer reimburse employees for charges put on their personal cards."

- **Step 5** *Make sure everyone understands you intend to enforce the new policy.* You would think by announcing the consequences of noncompliance, employees would get the message. Most will, but not everyone. Expect there will be at least one case, if not more, where employees will test you. In order to make the policy stick, you are going to have to refuse someone's charges on the personal card. For, if you don't, you'll have numerous employees ignoring the policy. However, if one or two employees end up eating charges put on personal cards, everyone will get the message.

- **Step 6** *Make sure everyone affected by the change is included in your communication.* This is especially true if you have admins who complete expense reimbursement reports for their bosses. Again, by including everyone in the distribution of the announcement of the policy change there are no loopholes employees can try and crawl through.

Implementing a change in policy is rarely an easy task. Using these simple guidelines will make the process just a little bit easier.

Using the Manual

Many professionals get full mileage from their policy and procedures manual by using it for multiple purposes. These include:

- As a training guide for new processors

- As a reference guide for current processors

- To provide directions to those interacting with the accounts payable department

"Our AP department has had a very detailed Policy & Procedure 'manual' for over six years. This organization publishes it on the company portal in the AP collaboration room," one manager explains. She concludes noting, "It is our 'bible'!"

Another organization takes a similar approach (and one we suspect is followed at many firms). The policy and procedures manual is stored online in a shared directory which everyone can access. Each procedure is in a folder related to the system or team that handles the process.

One of the practices advocated by AP Now is the manual be used both as a training and reference tool. Here's how one of the respondents does precisely that. They use the manual when they have interns for a small period of time. Instead of going through the procedure step by step with the intern, they simply give them the procedure manual. If the interns have questions, they can ask a staff member. She also notes that if something is not updated properly, they have the opportunity to correct it as things can change and update at any time.

Along the same lines, one of our readers explains how her organization uses the travel and expense portion of the manual. Some organizations include the travel policy with the accounts payable policy and procedures manual, while others have a separate document.] When there is an issue with an expense report, she takes a copy of the company policy that shows what the company will allow and highlights it. This is sent with the expense report back to the manager who approved the expense report to let them know the expense report cannot be reimbursed as submitted.

A number of professionals get nauseous at the thought of putting together a manual from scratch asking if there was a standard policies and procedure book they could purchase to use as a resource. There are a number of good books available on accounts payable topics. Just make sure to pick one with a recent publication date, i.e. after 2010.

Readers without manuals should take a look at their systems documentation for accounts payable processes. If it is done decently, this might provide a good starting point for your manual. Another good starting point are policies and procedures from other organizations. Many can be downloaded from the Internet. But, if you do that, take care. They will need serious modification to match the policies and procedures used in your organization.

Alternatives for Those Who Don't Have A Policy and Procedures Manual

When it comes to the accounts payable function, it is critical that everyone within the same organization handle the function in exactly that same way. In this manner, the number of duplicate payments likely to be made is kept to a bare minimum. In order for this to happen, most organizations rely on a detailed written policy and procedures manual. This document, almost always and an electronic file can be shared with everyone who needs the information. But putting together such a manual and keeping it updated can take a bit of work.

Is A Manual Really Necessary?

While this information is critical to a well-run accounts payable function, and for many a policy and procedures manual is the easiest way to collect and centralize the intelligence needed to run the function, some question the absolute imperative to have a manual. We surveyed accounts payable professionals on this issue and a few offered alternatives that seemed to work in their organizations. Here's a look at the best alternatives provided by our survey respondents.

- Though we don't have a 'manual', we do have procedures written and posted on a shared site for our company that include step by step processes for entry and FAQ's

- Our procedures are documented. Our company has policies related to AP in Procurement, Treasury, and Internal Control documents, but there are no global or local AP Policy documents.

- We don't have just one Policy & Procedure manual. We have Policy & Procedures or Work instructions for several areas. New Vendor set up, New customer set up, Month End AP, Month End AR, Year End 1099 Forms, Sales & Use tax set up and reporting, and about ten other work instructions for our accounting department.

- Because our company is frequently involved in acquisitions, the SAP Accounts Payable module utilized becomes the default manual.

- Our department has a Payables Process Memo which is a quick reference for auditors and others.

- Although we don't have a formal policy manual presently, the department is working on putting one together. In the meantime I have a memo which I give to new employees as well as sending it out once every fiscal year explaining the AP procedures and policies we have in place. This memo explains travel and reimbursement expensing and per diems as well as procedures for submitting invoices for payment etc.

- We had a loose collection of written procedures. For example, the procedure for a wire or for an ACH transaction.

- We do not have a manual per se, but some folders on a shared drive.

- We have a simple FAQ posted to the company' shared drive to help the employees with policy and procedure questions; we also have procedures for many of the AP functions but, since we only have one AP employee, they only get used if she is absent.

A Word about the Travel Policy

Some organizations include their travel policy in the accounts payable policy and procedures manual, but most have a separate travel policy. This is a good idea as the travel policy is shared with a large number of employees, most of whom have little interest in accounts payable.

This does not mean that you cannot have procedures for handling travel expenses included in the accounts payable policy and procedures manual; it simply means that there should be a separate document that is the travel policy. This separate document is the one shared with the entire organization.

While we still believe a policy and procedures manual is a recommended best practice, some of the alternatives discussed above do a pretty good job of emulating one. And, the rest, serve as an admirable stop gap until the time and resources are available to have one created.

CHAPTER 15
REGULATORY ISSUES AFFECTING THE ACCOUNTS PAYABLE FUNCTION

You don't need this book to know that the Feds and the IRS are quite intent on locating unreported income to help close the tax gap and many of the states are aggressively looking for every last dime to help shore up the shortfalls in their budgets. To make sure they get all the funds they are entitled to, all are putting increased pressure on companies and other entities to make sure they do everything they are supposed to in this regard. Whether this means reporting and remitting all the funds they owe or reporting the income paid to others, the pressure has been relentless and shows no sign of letting up.

Adding to the headache is the fact that not only is pressure revving up for compliance with existing regulatory issues; new ones are rearing their ugly heads. The information presented in this chapter is intended to introduce readers to the concepts and provide a rudimentary understanding of what needs to be done. It is in no way comprehensive. That would require hundreds of pages. In this chapter we'll take a look at:

- Information reporting (Forms 1099 and 1042)
- Unclaimed Property (escheat)
- Sales and Use Tax
- Foreign Corrupt Practices Act (FCPA)

- OFAC Reporting
- Regulatory Mistakes Every Organization Should Avoid

Tax Information Reporting

According to the IRS, any person, including a corporation, partnership, individual, estate, and trust, making reportable transactions during the calendar year must file information returns to report those transactions to the IRS. Persons required to file information returns to the IRS must also furnish statements to the recipients of the income. Filers who have 250 or more must file these returns electronically.

Transactions reportable on a Form 1099-MISC are as follows (with the most common items being highlighted although all must be reported):

What Gets Reported on a 1099-MISC

- Attorneys, fees and gross proceeds
- Auto reimbursements, non-employee
- Awards, non-employee
- Bonuses, non-employee
- Car expense, non-employee
- Commissions, non-employee
- Compensation, non-employee
- Crop insurance proceeds
- Damages
- Direct sales of consumer products for resale
- Directors' fees
- Fees, non-employee
- Fishing boat crew members proceeds
- Fish purchases for cash
- Golden parachute, non-employee
- Health care services
- Indian gaming profits paid to tribal members
- Medical services
- Mileage, non-employee
- Non-employee compensation
- Prizes, non-employee
- Punitive damages
- Rents
- Royalties

- Substitute payments in lieu of dividends or tax-exempt interest

The information must be sent to the recipient by January 31 and to the IRS by February 28.

The determination of who gets a 1099 is made on the basis of the recipients' classification. If the recipient is to get a 1099, then his or her taxpayer identification number (TIN) is required. For individuals this is the social security number. It is highly recommended that the IRS Form W-9 be used for this purpose, although at the current time this isn't mandatory.

1099s and W-9s are for payments to U.S. persons only. If a payment is made to a contractor who is a nonresident alien, different rules and forms apply.

When 1099s Are Handled Incorrectly

The consequences of handling tax information reporting requirements incorrectly can be quite severe. In addition to dealing with headache-inducing B Notices, six months to a year after the initial reporting, there can be penalties and fines for getting the information wrong. While there are limits on the amount of these fines, if a determination is made that the organization intentionally disregarded the rules the limits no longer apply.

This is an area that has come under increased scrutiny from tax regulators and auditors, which in all likelihood will continue.

Best TIN Solicitation Practices

The following are not difficult to do as long as everyone gets on board.

- Get a W-9 from everyone with whom you do business before you make your first payment. Refuse to make the payment until a signed W-9 is received and verified.

- Sign up for the IRS TIN Matching program—and use it.

- Verify the TIN information provided before making that first payment. If you get a mismatch, you can get corrected information while you still hold the trump card.

That's it: just three simple steps. By following them you will dramatically reduce the number of errors and B-Notices. And there's another bonus. By following these steps you will be able to demonstrate to the IRS—should there be a problem—that you, in good faith, did the required due diligence. This will go a long way towards having penalties and fines abated.

Unclaimed Property: The Basics of Escheat Reporting and Remitting

Unclaimed property, also referred to as escheat or abandoned property, is defined as the reversion of property to the state or county, as provided by state law, when the property is abandoned. How you define abandoned and how the state does may be two very different things. As you probably realize, it's only what the state thinks that matters.

Property holders must turn over unclaimed property to the states, a process that affects every organization, whether it be for profit or not-for-profit. That's right, most nonprofits need to comply. For most of our readers, the main categories of unclaimed property include:

- Uncashed vendor checks;

- Uncashed payroll checks (this often happens when an employee leaves and moves concurrently); and

- Open credits.

Financial institutions have additional responsibilities for what are considered abandoned bank accounts and securities but a discussion of those issues is beyond the scope of this publication.

Complying organizations must report to each state annually. All the states do not have the same deadline—that might make the process too easy. The majority of the states have a November 1 deadline, with March 1 being the filing date for another large group of the states. These filings must be done on time, as the states typically have a penalty for late filing in addition to the fine for non-filers!

Minimizing Unclaimed Property

Some companies like to hold onto uncashed checks eventually writing them off their books to miscellaneous income. This is a really bad idea. Since the funds related to uncashed vendor checks have to be turned over to the state and you don't get to keep the money, why not try to improve vendor relations by tracking down the vendors to whom you owe the money and give them their funds?

The recommended policy is simple: Have as few checks left outstanding as possible. This means systematically following up on all uncashed checks on a regular basis, not just at the end of the year. You can't hold onto the funds so you may as well give them to their rightful owner.

In addition to researching uncashed checks to ensure that the funds end up in the hands of the rightful property owners, companies should establish rigid procedures for their payment processes as well as other accounts payable functions. Not only will this ensure a well-run operation, minimize (if not eliminate) duplicate payments, and make fraud more difficult, they will help the company minimize unnecessary escheatment.

The Dilemma for Those Currently Not in Compliance

It's a well-known but little-discussed fact that not every organization complies with the unclaimed property laws. Most experts believe only about one-third of those who should comply actually do. But increasingly those that are not in compliance with the escheat laws (the legal terminology) are reconsidering that stance—either of their own accord or more likely, because a state auditor has shown up on their doorstep. Once they decide to get in compliance, they need to do so gingerly.

From time to time different states will offer amnesty on this issue. But before you decide to bite the bullet and take advantage of one of these offers, read the fine print very carefully. It is unlikely that you will just be able to start complying going forward. Typically these offers are for amnesty of fines for past noncompliance, not for the amounts that you should have escheated.

If you are not currently in compliance, there are several ways to begin complying. You could:

- Do it yourself (not recommended).
- Have a firm do it for you at no cost as some will (really not recommended).
- Hire a firm to get you in compliance.

This is an issue that is very sensitive. If the state gets wind that you are not in compliance, they will be in for an audit before your expert has a chance to approach them and negotiate a settlement.

A Word about the No-Cost Option

As noted above, there are some firms that will get you in compliance at no cost to you the first year. If at first glance, this seems like an attractive option, consider the fact that I refer to this approach as the penny-wise-pound-foolish way of getting into compliance. As Kurt Vonnegut was fond of saying, there's no such thing as a free lunch. These firms are compensated by the states on a contingency basis; they have no incentive to work to reduce your escheatable items. Also, a large payment now sets the stage for larger payments on an ongoing basis.

No matter what you think about the escheat laws, you *are* required to turn over unclaimed property to the states. It's the law. If not currently in compliance, consider the facts and alternatives presented here and proceed with a well-considered plan.

Sales and Use Tax Basics

Sales and use tax is another of those specialty topics that sometimes falls under the accounts payable umbrella and other times in the tax department. Very large organizations typically have separate sales and use tax departments. Like unclaimed property, it is one of those areas that the states have seized upon as an income resource. A number of the states have been aggressively pursing corporations that are not reporting correctly. With over 7,000—yes, that's correct, 7,000—separate taxing entities, proper reporting can be a monumental task for any organization operating in more than one or two different taxing entities.

Definition of Sales and Use Tax

Sales tax is a charge on the retail sale of tangible personal property. It is important to note that it should be paid only on retail sales. It is also levied on certain services. Use tax is a little more complicated. It is charged by many (but not all) states on the "privilege of storing." In this case, storage means the purchaser's holding or controlling property brought in from out of state that is not intended for resale. Generally speaking, if goods are to be used for demonstration or display, they are not subject to use tax. The rules for what is and is not subject to use tax are very complicated and vary from state to state. So it's essential that the AP professionals responsible for sales and use tax learn what their state rules are.

A few companies have no formal policies and procedures for the sales and use tax responsibility. An auditor who finds a company in noncompliance is likely to be more sympathetic to a company that has a policy in place than one who has ignored the issue. The existence of a policy indicates that the company intends to pay its sales and use taxes, even if it doesn't always do it correctly. The lack of a formal policy implies that the company has no plan to pay. Thus, the existence of a policy is a company's first defense against an aggressive tax collector.

Even those with a policy need to revise and update it periodically as the laws continually change. Finally, there is one last reason to have a policy in place—the communication that goes on among states and among the different taxing authorities within one state. Many in the field believe this information is freely exchanged. Once a company is hit for back payments and penalties, the likelihood is that other taxing authorities will come knocking at their door.

Nexus

You should be aware that any of the following *could* trigger nexus:

- Ownership in the form of inventory or equipment.

- Ownership of a billboard.

- Maintenance by a company of a building (office, warehouse, retail store, etc.).

- Lease or rental facilities.

- Presence of an affiliate (parent or subsidiary).

- Participation in a trade show.

- And in recent years, there has been a whole specter of new issues related to click-through nexus, based on Internet transactions.

Remember, with nexus comes sales and use tax responsibilities.

Foreign Corrupt Practices Act Compliance

Many readers probably know the Foreign Corrupt Practices Act (FCPA) prohibits bribing foreign government officials and they may wonder how this impacts the accounts payable function. After all, no one in accounts payable will be in a position to initiate a bribe of a foreign government official. And, this is most decidedly true. However, accounts payable is the last set of eyes to see a transaction before the money goes out the door. Therefore, it is imperative that they review payments for potential violations. It is also why many experts now recommend that employees be given some training in this area.

Background

In mid-seventies, an SEC investigation found over 400 companies admitted to making questionable or illegal payments in excess of $300 million for the purpose of securing favorable action by foreign governments.

As you might imagine, many of these transactions did not cast a favorable light on the companies that made the payments and Americans in general. As a result, FCPA legislation was passed in 1977 and *all* US companies doing business outside US must be familiar with it.

In the last ten years or so, there have been several large cases where the organizations involved received a lot of bad press and paid large fines for violating this law. This has raised the profile of the issue.

Basics of FCPA

Simply put, FCPA prohibits corrupt payments to foreign officials or the purpose of gaining or keeping business. While it sounds simple enough, it is anything but. There are exceptions discussed later in this piece. The Act is enforced by Department of Justice for criminal and civil enforcements and the SEC for civil enforcement with respect to issuers of securities.

What Constitutes a Violation?

When trying to determine if you have a potential violation, examine the following five factors.

- **Factor #1** Who does the act apply to? Any of the following individuals acting on behalf of the firm:

    - Individual

    - Firm

    - Officer

    - Director

    - Employee

    - Agent of the firm

    - Individuals or firms who order, authorize or assist someone else in violating the Act

- **Factor #2** Is there corrupt intent? Is the party involved trying to get the recipient to misuse his/her official position to direct business wrongly to your company or another. Note: To be guilty, you don't have to be successful!

- **Factor #3.** Examine the payment. Not only can't you pay, offer to pay or promise to pay, you can't authorize others to pay. And that payment can be money or anything else of value. This is where T&E can play a role.

• **Factor #4** Examine the recipient. This is where it can bet really tricky. Payments (for FCPA purposes) should not be made to any of the following:

1. Foreign official
2. Officer, employee of
3. Foreign government
4. Public international organizations
5. Department or agency (of the above)
6. Any person acting in an official capacity
7. Foreign political party
8. Party official
9. Candidate for foreign political office

• **Factor #5** Does it meet the business purpose test? FCPA references "obtaining or retaining business." This is interpreted broadly and refers to both the awarding of new business as well as the renewal of existing business.

One Last Caveat

Do not try and find a way around the legislation. No payments may be made through third-party intermediaries. Simply put; if you know that a portion of the payment will be used for corrupt purposes, you cannot make it.

Please also be aware that as far as the SEC and DOJ are concerned with this legislation, knowing includes "conscious disregard and deliberate ignorance." Every organization affected by this legislation is expected to know and understand its requirements and ramifications and make sure their employees abide by it.

Bribery under FCPA

When most people think of bribery they think of the exchange of money as the medium of exchange. But, this does not have to be, especially when talking about the Foreign Corrupt Practices Act (FCPA), In fact, the Act defines a bribe very broadly as "anything of value." So in addition to money, this might include:

- An offer of employment for the recipient or someone designated by the recipient
- Discounts
- Gifts
- Lavish meals and other entertainment (including trips)
- Stock
- A commission
- Property

What's more, the bribe is still a bribe if it is paid through a third party or is a future payment. These considerations make it all the more difficult for accounts payable to ferret out payments that are really bribes. It is also why it is important to scrutinize expense reimbursements closely

Exceptions

As mentioned earlier, there are a few exceptions to these rules. They include facilitating payments for routine government actions including:

- Obtaining permits, licenses or other official documents
- Processing government papers (e.g. visas, work orders)
- Providing police protection
- Mail pick-up and delivery
- Providing phone service, power and water supply
- Loading and unloading cargo
- Protecting perishable products

- Scheduling inspections associated with contract performance or transit of goods

What This Means for AP

For starters, at all affected companies, the staff should understand what is expected by FCPA. This is not intuitive or something that is normally part of training for the accounts payable function. This means that there should be some special training for the accounts payable staff. There should be written procedures which can be included in policy and procedures manual.

The staff should also be alerted to the fact that if they find a possible FCPA violation, it should be brought to management's attention for handling. This needs to be addressed at a higher level. The staff should be warned to expect many false positives. You will find quite a few questionable payments that upon further investigation will turn out to be perfectly legitimate transactions.

The Basics of OFAC Checking

The Office of Foreign Assets Control (OFAC) of the US Department of the Treasury administers and enforces economic and trade sanctions based on US foreign policy and national security goals. It prohibits payments to targeted foreign countries, terrorists, international narcotics traffickers, and those engaged in activities related to the proliferation of weapons of mass destruction.

Impact on the Payment Function

Every organization in the US must comply with OFAC regulations. This includes all U.S. citizens and permanent resident aliens regardless of where they are located, all persons and entities within the United States, all U.S. incorporated entities and their foreign branches. In the cases of certain programs, such as those regarding Cuba and North Korea, all foreign subsidiaries owned or controlled by U.S. companies also must comply. Fines for violations can be substantial.

OFAC publishes a list of individuals and companies owned or controlled by, or acting for or on behalf of, targeted countries.

It also lists individuals, groups, and entities, such as terrorists and narcotics traffickers designated under programs that are not country-specific. Collectively, such individuals and companies are called "Specially Designated Nationals" or SDN. Their assets are blocked and U.S. persons are generally prohibited from dealing with them.

There are thousands of names on the list. What's more, the list is regularly updated with new names. The best way to get the list is from OFAC's website at

http://www.treasury.gov/about/organizational-structure/offices/Pages/Office-of-Foreign-Assets-Control.aspx

If you have checked a name and find a match, don't be alarmed. This is another time when you will find a lot of false positives. Do a little more research. By becoming familiar with the regulations pertaining to payments to SDNs, accounts payable professionals can protect their companies against stiff penalties.

Unfortunately, this is not a one-time task. In reality, before every payment is made, the list should be checked. Not many are up to the task. Some check the list when they set up new vendors in the master vendor file. Others run their whole master vendor file against the OFAC list once a month. Some of the new vendor portals have the ability to automatically do this checking before each check run. It's just one more way the accounts payable function is evolving.

Silly Regulatory Mistakes Every Organization Should Avoid

It's so easy to get into regulatory hot water, it's not funny. This is especially true when it comes to the issues that affect accounts payable. Let's take a look at seven of the most common mistakes made, along with simple solutions on how to avoid them. Sometimes just identifying the issue is enough, but where more advice is required, we'll include it. We'll start with the newest issue – and one that is starting to attract attention in the form of lawsuits being filed by those who feel they have been wronged.

- **Mistake #1** Having unpaid interns do clerical work previously done by paid employees and not having an educational component to their apprenticeship. The Department of Labor (DOL) has guidelines companies are supposed to follow when they hire interns. With the recent downturn in the economy, many organizations have expanded their use of interns, often forgetting the guidelines set by the DOL. If your organization hires interns it is imperative that it be a learning situation for the intern and not just a way for your organization to get some free or very-low-cost labor.

- **Mistake #2** Adding sales tax to an invoice for an item that requires sales tax. Typically the reason for not including the sales tax is it is an out-of-state vendor who does not have nexus in your state. Adding sales tax to an invoice will not get the tax paid. It will simply get you a credit with the vendor and trouble with the sales tax auditors when they show up. You will then be required to pay the use tax you were supposed to accrue (plus any penalties) and be left on your own to recoup your overpayment to the vendor. Call the vendor and find out why they did not include the sales tax.

- **Mistake #3** Paying sales/use tax or remitting unclaimed property to the wrong state. Sometimes organizations feel it would be much easier to make all their payments to one state rather than make payments to numerous states. And they are correct; it is easier but not right. When the state that should have received the money comes knocking on their door, they are going to have to pay that state and will then be left on their own to recoup the original payment from the state it was paid incorrectly to. And, that is not likely to be a fun situation. So, send your money to the state that is supposed to get it, not the one that it is easiest to send it to.

- **Mistake #4** Writing off uncashed checks to miscellaneous income. This tactic, quite common a decade ago, has gotten more than a few organizations into hot water when the unclaimed property auditors show up. How do they find it? One of the first items auditors will look at is the miscellaneous income account – and they will want complete documentation for everything it in. If you don't have it, get ready to write a check to the state. Follow the correct due diligence procedures for uncashed checks.

- **Mistake #5** Not issuing all the Form 1099s an organization should. Many firms send out W-9s and then hope that they get them all back. Few get 100% response. Others rely on the "eyeball test" thinking that because an organization has Inc. in its title, it is a corporation. Unfortunately, that is not always true. Both of these practices will lead the organization to issue fewer Form 1099s than they should. When the organization is subject to an Information Reporting audit and it becomes apparent that additional Forms 1099 should have been issued, it is penalty and fine time. If you are not already doing so, begin tracking who you sent Form W-9s to and who returned it. Follow up with those who have not returned theirs.

- **Mistake #6** Using DBA on 1099s. If you use the DBA on Forms 1099 instead of the legal business name of the entity, you will get a name/TIN (taxpayer identification number) mismatch from the IRS in the form of those dreaded B-Notices. Your best approach is to run your information through IRS TIN Matching and find this out before you issue your Forms 1099. Then you've got time to fix the information and avoid a B-Notice nightmare. And remember, always use the legal name on the Forms 1099.

- **Mistake #7** Letting management or any executive classify returning executives as independent contractors. Sometimes an agreement will be made with a new hire that they will be treated as an independent contractor. This is not the correct way to handle this issue. Worker classification (whether someone is an employee or independent contractor) is heating up to be a big issue. The decision is not one that management or anyone in your company should be making. It is dictated by guidelines set down by the IRS. Get it wrong and there can be severe financial consequences. You should also be aware that the IRS has a form (SS-8) that can be filled out by any one working for your firm as an independent contractor asking the IRS to evaluate whether they should have been classified as an employee. If you are not certain, fill out the form yourself and have the IRS make the final decision.

Many of the regulatory mistakes discussed above are not made by an organization trying to play games or avoid financial responsibility. They are made out of a less than complete understanding of the law. This is one place where education can go a long way. For remember, ignorance of the law is no excuse for not abiding by it. That's the position the auditors will take when assessing fines and/or penalties.

CHAPTER 16
USING TECHNOLOGY TO RUN A MORE EFFICIENT ACCOUNTS PAYABLE FUNCTION

Without a doubt, technology has impacted just about every facet of the business process, and the procure-to-pay process is no exception. Creative employees have found numerous ways to make technology work for them in ways never imagined just a few short years ago. This chapter takes a look at some of the innovative ways they have done this. Specifically, it examines:

- Low-cost Technology Approaches

- Integrating Internal Controls with Your Technology

- Using Technology to Minimize Duplicate Payments

- A Few Excel Quick Tricks for a More Efficient Accounts Payable Function

Electronic Accounts Payable: Simple Tactics Any Company Can Use

Perhaps the biggest change to the accounts payable function over the last few years is the rate that it is being automated. I'm not just talking about big company high-dollar automation projects. We're also talking about low-dollar, process changes that every company can implement without spending a fortune—and in many cases without spending a single red cent. Let's take a look at some of these strategies.

1)   Get rid of paper invoices. Next to paper checks, paper invoices are the biggest time consumer in accounts payable. And that doesn't even address the issue of storage. Even if you don't sign up for a third party e-invoicing service, you can accept invoices by email. Many suppliers are refusing to mail invoices and accepting them by email should be a no-brainer. Don't give back your savings by printing the invoices once they arrive in your shop. Establish standard procedures for processing them without the paper.

2)   Eliminate those paper faxed invoices and other faxes by signing up for a low cost e-fax facility that converts your paper faxes to emails so you never again get a fax delivered on paper. This is another tactic that will help eliminate paper invoices from the accounts payable department.

3)   When you have to send documents, either for approval or because there is a dispute, don't make copies and mail them. Scan the documents and attach them to emails for discussion or resolution. Of course, if you received the documents electronically, you won't have to scan them.

4)   Encourage vendors to accept payments via the ACH instead of receiving paper checks. This will not only reduce the amount of paper, it will save tons of processing time – and of course, save a few trees. Best of all ACH payments are cheaper than issuing a paper check and rarely result in an unclaimed property obligation.

5)   Insist on ACH for all employee reimbursements for expenses. While most states won't allow you to mandate electronic payments for payroll, you can insist on reimbursing employees for expenses this way.

6)   Make payments to vendors electronically. This will help get rid of those awful paper checks and all

the problems associated with them. And, not only will you get rid of some of the paper, electronic payments are cheaper than paper checks.

7)   Email your vendors receiving ACH payments their remittance information. If you can find an effective way to do this, more vendors will sign up for your ACH program, eliminating even more of those awful paper checks. One of the main reasons suppliers are reluctant to sign up for ACH is the lack of information usually included on the remittance advice and used to apply cash. If you can find a way to deliver that needed information to the person responsible for applying cash, you will have won that battle.

8)   Only make Rush payments using the ACH. Do not issue checks outside the normal check production schedule. This can be a tough one but once the vendor receives the payment in their bank account the very next day, they will find they like it and may switch to receiving all payments from you electronically. Paying via the ACH will eliminate some—but not all—of the problems associated with Rush checks.

9)   Send an e-mail with explanations of short payments to vendors, if information doesn't fit on remittance advice. The beauty of this approach is by taking the initiative you not only improve vendor relationships; you also reduce the number of calls coming into accounts payable.

10)   Purchase a low-cost simple scanner for use in handling those documents that do arrive in paper format. Scan the invoices before distributing them to your processors for handling. Let them learn to process invoices without relying on that piece of paper. This will make it easier if you go one day to a third party e-invoicing process. And, it will save on storage.

11)   Set up a Coding Matrix. A lot of work that ends up in accounts payable really should be done elsewhere. However, the reality is the task ends up

in accounts payable and the professionals who work there have to find a way to handle it. One such example is GL coding. While we believe the person who initiated a purchase or approved an invoice for payment is in the best position to know where an item should be coded in the GL, the task often falls to the processors. Create a "Coding Matrix" for commonly used vendors. The matrix gives the AP processors information on the approval workflow as well as the GL account coding (by vendor). The matrix can be stored online on the department site and is continually updated as needed.

An Internal Control Plan to Help You Use Technology to Run an Efficient AP Operation

Without a doubt, technology can help managers run a more efficient operation. However, and equally troubling, if not used properly it can also increase the likelihood of duplicate payments and make it easier for fraudsters to get their hands on some of your organization's cash. Not taking advantage of technology is clearly not the answer. So what can you do to minimize the risks while still making appropriate use of the advances on the market? Try this 12-step plan:

1. Insist on appropriate internal controls. Often overlooked, especially in the development of new approaches, internal controls are key to ensuring fraud does not happen. It is also important when areas other than accounts payable initiate payments, as frequently happens with p-cards, wire transfers, and ACH payment. It is imperative under these circumstances that one payment file is updated and the information is entered on a very timely basis. Otherwise, duplicate payments will skyrocket as invoices show up in accounts payable for items paid for by other departments. Similarly, if you are using ERS and the vendor cannot suppress the printing of the invoice, strong controls are needed to ensure the invoices are not paid.

2. Proper segregation of duties should be incorporated into every procedure not only within the accounts payable department but within the company. One frequently overlooked area is the master vendor file. Responsibility

for entering new vendors and updating information on existing ones needs to be segregated from anyone with the ability to create a PO, place an order, receive goods and update the receiving information, process or approve invoices, and/or handle checks. Thus, depending on the size of the accounts payable and procurement departments, this function can sometimes end up in another accounting area.

3. Demand processors use pre-set coding standards. This is important to avoid duplicate payments. It is especially so when it comes to entering the invoice number. Often controllers or managers confidently tell me they believe their organizations make few duplicate payments because their system will not accept the same invoice number twice. Then when I talk to their processors, they confide that they get around that restriction by simply adding a blank space or a period or something else to trick the system. So much for the effectiveness of that control.

4. Do not permit processors to develop their own workarounds. When everyone does not process in the same manner, differences creep in and ultimately permit duplicate payments to slip through. Inevitably, after working with invoices day after day processors begin to find "better" ways to do things. And, the truth of the matter is, sometimes these new ways are better, although at other times the so-called improvements lack the appropriate internal controls needed or cause more work to another party. Processors who find better ways to handle the work flow should be encouraged to share their thoughts with their supervisors. If indeed, they have found an improved process then everyone on the team can benefit.

5. Check for duplicate payments. Technology makes it easier than ever to check for duplicate payments. Many of the latest releases of ERP software have duplicate payment checking routines. By using these modules you can identify duplicates before the payment leaves your shop. If these modules are not available, develop routines using Excel or Access to check for duplicates.

Unfortunately, many organizations do not activate those modules.

6. Do your own simple check to uncover fraud. While many executives do not like to admit that their employees would steal from them, the unvarnished truth is, occasionally, it happens. One quick way to identify such fraud is to run the employee address file against the addresses in the master vendor file to identify matches. Before you do this make sure to adjust for employee addresses in the master vendor file for T&E reimbursement purposes. Then research any matches. While occasionally there is a legitimate reason for a match, it is one easy way to uncover sloppy employee fraud.

7. Document procedures and then do a surprise audit. By documenting the processes there is a record to be used for training and to ensure that everyone continues to process in the same manner. Periodically audit processors to ensure they are still operating within the approved procedures. By monitoring staff on a surprise basis, there is no opportunity for the processor to check the book before you show up and revert back to the approved procedures.

8. Don't overlook your desktop applications in your assessments. When assessing for internal controls, consistency in processing, or fraud potential, do not overlook the desktop applications. Often organizations with the very best processes forget about those control concerns when desktop applications are being developed.

9. Generate variance reporting to measure and identify potential problems. Technology makes generating reports simpler. Develop reports that identify variances so you can pinpoint potential problem and fraud areas. By knowing which processors are putting in the most adjustments you can determine if additional training is needed or if something fishy is going on. Similarly, check to see which vendors are generating the most changes. Is it something in the way their invoices are prepared or is there a problem on your end?

10. Clean up the master vendor file. Without a doubt, messy master vendor files provide an opportunity for anyone with a fraudulent bent. Not to mention that they are also a cause for duplicate payments. Cleaning up the master vendor file will require some manual effort. However, with the right reports, you can hire a temp or use lower-level clerical people for this task. The master vendor file information can be dumped into an Excel file and scrubbed.

11. Hire a duplicate payment auditor working on a contingency basis. Even the most conscientious organization employing best practices will still occasionally make duplicate or other erroneous payments—although not nearly as many as an organization with weak controls and poor processes. The hiring of a duplicate payment audit recovery firm is not an admission of wrongdoing but rather a sign of a smart operator. After all, it's your money——why shouldn't you try and hold on to as much of it as you possibly can?

12. Don't be afraid of new technology and other advances available to improve the payment process. The changes coming into the payment space are amazing. Techniques that were on the bleeding edge just a few short years ago are now common place. Evaluate new proposals as they come your way and decide whether or not they will enhance your operations.

Most of these steps just make good common sense. Yet, it is amazing how many organizations don't utilize them. This is a 12-step program we heartily endorse.

Using Technology to Minimize Duplicate Payments

Most organizations have made great strides in eradicating duplicate payments. They insist on stringent coding standards, regularly cleanse their master vendor file and have standardized their invoice handling processes. While these actions certainly will make a big dent in the duplicate payment issue, they won't completely eliminate the problem. The following three steps, which rely heavily on technology, will help identify those invoices that still slip through a second time, despite the best practices you've already integrated into your process.

> • **Step 1**. Rely on the invoice number limitation that prevents the entering of a duplicate invoice number in your ERP system, if it has that capability. For this tool to do full duty, it is critical that your invoice processors understand the importance of entering the invoice number correctly and not monkeying around with it, if it shows as a duplicate. Too often, processors simply modify the invoice number slightly to force an invoice through. In reality, the fact that the ERP system is signaling the item as a duplicate should be a red flag that it is likely a duplicate invoice.

> • **Step 2.** Use duplicate payment checking routines inherent in your ERP system before payments are released. Too often this functionality is turned off or was never turned on, when the system was first installed. This is unfortunate because the organization has paid for functionality that is not being used and could save thousands or millions of dollars.

> • **Step 3.** Create simple Excel routines to check for duplicate payments before the payments are released. These can be created using the conditional formatting function and are relatively easy to run. This checking is especially important when running checks at the beginning of a new fiscal year or when there has been a system upgrade or a migration to a new system. All these events are likely to trigger an increase in potential duplicate payments. So, this extra checking is well worth the time involved in the task.

While your good practices throughout the procure-to-pay process combined with the routines suggested above will certainly help identify duplicate payments before the payments leaves your door, a few will still slip though. That's where statement audits can help. Conduct these audits on a very regular basis.

They are the best way to ensure you have collected all your vendor credits, some of which may have been created by duplicate payments. If you don't have the time or resources necessary to handle complete statement audits of all your vendors, have a third party firm conduct one for you.

Excel Tactics to Improve AP Efficiency

It's hard to imagine working in accounts payable without a desktop computer, e-mail and Excel. Luckily, we don't have to face that prospect anymore. When it comes to Excel's role, there are numerous tactics anyone can use to help them reach the goal of a smoother accounts payable function. Let's look at five of the simpler tactics. They include:

1) Use the conditional formatting feature to find duplicate payments and duplicate vendors in the master vendor file.

2) Dump T&E expense reimbursement line date into an into an Excel spreadsheet and search for:

   a. Items just under the receipt level
   b. Duplicate items (same dollar amount)
   c. Same receipt on two expense reports or on two employees

3) Put the addresses from your master vendor file into an Excel spreadsheet and match them against the addresses from your HR file, using conditional formatting. Research any duplicates to uncover employees masquerading as fraudulent vendors and/or inappropriate hiring of spouses or family members as consultants. This is important if your organization has a policy forbidding such hiring or it was not disclosed.

4) Similarly, run employee social security numbers against the TINs supplied by vendors. Investigate any matches to determine if there is inappropriate activity.

5) Produce analytical data that purchasing can use to negotiate better contracts for the organization. Use Excel to analyze purchasing data and identify:

a. Items purchased in quantity from several different vendors, perhaps by several different units;

b. Items purchased by different units at different prices; and/or

c. Unusually large amounts of an item purchased without a discount.

CHAPTER 17
INTERNAL CONTROLS: THE GLUE THAT HOLDS THE AP FUNCTION TOGETHER

If the accounts payable function is not handled properly, the viability of the whole organization is at risk. More than one company has gone bankrupt because the accounts payable function was ignored and someone took advantage or weak controls to rob the company blind. Accounts payable holds the control of the organization's pocketbook and as such, it is imperative that strong internal controls be integrated across the function. For if they are not the results can be catastrophic. In this section, we take a look at:

- Importance of the Control Issue
- Segregation of Duties
- Internal Control Breakdowns

Why Internal Controls Are So Important

Let's face it; if you've worked in accounts payable or another accounting area for more than a few weeks you understand the importance of strong internal controls. Yet, more than a few organizations allow their controls to weaken. The possible problems related to flawed internal controls fall into three areas:

- Fraud
- Duplicate Payments

- Regulatory Non-Compliance

Let's examine the potential fallout from each of these issues.

Fraud

This is the obstacle most think of when the matter of weak controls is raised. Without a doubt weak internal controls make it easier for anyone to perpetrate a fraud. It is important to realize that fraud is not only a risk from outsiders, you also have internal issues.

Unfortunately, the group of people who knows best where your control weaknesses are, are your employees. While most would never dream of taking advantage of that knowledge, a few would. Not only do they know where the potential loopholes are they know how to exploit them.

Weakened internal controls that lead to process problems have another unintended ramification. More than a few frauds start with an honest mistake. Maybe a vendor sent a second invoice because you paid a discrepant invoice late. And if your processes aren't perfect, a second payment was made. This causes a light to go off at the less-than-scrupulous vendor who realizes your processes aren't what they should be. So, the supplier in question starts sending second and sometimes third invoices regularly.

Another common example of an honest mistake leading to an ongoing fraud is the employee who mistakenly submits the same expense on two different expense reports. When he or she realizes that the expense was paid twice, a light goes off. They quickly figure out they can (and they subsequently do) submit the same expense multiple times.

Duplicate Payments

The prevention of both duplicate payments and fraud go hand in hand. What you do to stop one will almost always do double duty. So, it should be no surprise to readers to learn that weak internal controls are also likely to lead to duplicate payments.

As most readers are aware, and unfortunately few outside the accounts payable/accounting function realize, few vendors return those excess payments. They deposit them and leave them for investigation at a later point. When that occurs, some issue credit memos for the duplicate payment.

This is where the matter gets a little tricky. Even if the vendor issued the credit memo, accounts payable may or may not get it. This is for a variety of reasons, and is one of the numerous reasons why AP Now strongly recommends regular statement audits looking for open vendor credits.

But let's say the vendor does issue the credit memo and it makes it to your accounts payable department. In most of these cases the credit memo is used appropriately. But in a few processors don't recognize the credit memo and thinking it is an invoice, they pay it. That's why it is crucial all processers are trained to recognize credit memos and know how to handle them.

The remaining issue when discussing duplicate payments is what happens to those open credits if the customer doesn't claim them. In theory, after a few years, they should be turned over to the states as unclaimed property. This only happens in a small fraction of the cases. In reality, the professional charged with the accounts receivable function at your vendor will use them to cover accrued but unpaid late fees, unearned early payment discounts taken, or disputed invoices. "But wait," you say, "we have a policy of not paying those things."

That may very well be the case, but you won't be consulted on the matter. It will just happen and your open credits will vanish into thin air. That's another reason why frequent statement audits are strongly recommended.

Regulatory Non-compliance

For many, the mention of internal controls triggers thoughts of the Sarbanes-Oxley (S-Ox) Act and the requirement for the certification of strong internal controls. And there's good reason for that. But it should not be the only regulatory concern when it comes to internal controls.

When controls are weak not only is the required certification for S-Ox in jeopardy, but so is the ability to conform to a whole slew of other regulatory issues. If controls are tight and needed information recorded, the ability to conform to the laws related to issues like 1099 reporting, accrual of use tax, independent contractor classification, and unclaimed property requirements will be in jeopardy.

This hidden cost of less-than-ideal internal controls should not be underestimated. The expense and aggravation associated with an audit of any of the issues mentioned above can be quite high.

As you can probably figure out, all the issues in all three categories affect the productivity of the accounts payable function and the profitability of the organization as a whole in a negative way. Don't overlook any of them when evaluating the cost of weak controls across your procure-to-pay process.

Segregation of Duties: The Backbone of A Strong Internal Control Process

The segregation of duties concept is simple enough. Implementation is a different story. In order to perpetrate a fraud through accounts payable, it is frequently necessary to have access to more than one function. For example, a person would have to have access to the check stock and the facsimile signer. Thus, one of the easiest ways to prevent fraud is to assign responsibilities in such a manner to minimize this risk. Depending on the size of the department, it may be necessary to work with another group to achieve this goal. The accompanying chart spells out some standard segregation of duties as they apply to accounts payable.

Alternatively, close scrutiny on a regular basis of any person with multiple conflicting responsibilities is recommended. Companies sometimes get lulled into a false sense of security because the particular employee with multiple conflicting responsibilities has been with them a long time. This is a mistake, as most frauds are committed by long-time trusted employees.

The Common Problem

All too often an organization diligently sets up its procedures to ensure appropriate segregation of duties and then shoots itself in the foot by giving one or two people access to all tasks. The rationale for this varies. Sometimes a manager wants to make sure he or she can step in and train or fill in whenever needed.

In other cases, high-level executives feel they should have access to all information and functions.

The reasoning in both cases is faulty. No one should have access to everything—no matter how trusted an employee. Remember, most internal frauds are committed by long-term, trusted, employees.

If there is conflict over this issue, invite the auditors to weigh in and explain why the segregation is necessary.

Sample Segregation of Duties Chart

The person responsible for bank reconciliation should not:

- Handle unclaimed property reporting;
- Be a signer on a bank account.

The person who is a check signer should not:

- Authorize an invoice for payment on an account on which he/she is also a signer;
- Have ready access to the check stock.

A person who is responsible for the check stock should not:

- Be an authorized signer;
- Handle the bank reconciliations.

The person who is responsible for the master vendor file should not:

- Be an authorized signer;
- Be able to approve invoices for payment;
- Handle unclaimed property.

The person responsible for unclaimed property should not:

- Have responsibility for bank reconciliation;
- Have access to the master vendor file.

It Matters So Much

Whenever the topic of internal controls is raised, inevitably the issue of appropriate segregation of duties is raised. It is sometimes called separation of duties. In government the related concept is that of checks and balances. It is the theory of having several people completing a task with no one person responsible for the entire operation. This is one strategy to help prevent fraud.

Implications for Accounts Payable

When we talk about segregation of duties in accounts payable, we actually extend the concept to the entire procure-to-pay function (P2P). The idea is that no person can handle more than one leg in the P2P process. This makes collusion necessary to perpetrate certain frauds thereby making it harder for those few employees trying to play games and get money they are not entitled to.

Alas, this can be problematic in smaller departments as there are not enough employees to adequately incorporate a full segregation of duties. Under these circumstances there are two options as follows:

> 1) Most typically, certain tasks have to go elsewhere; or

> 2) Additional checks are built into the process to ensure there's no fraud.

What Gets Moved

The most common task that ends up leaving accounts payable is responsibility for the master vendor file. If the purchasing staff isn't sufficiently large enough either, then master vendor file sometimes ends up in another area in accounting. While it's nice to have it in accounts payable, that is not the critical issue.

What is key is that it is handled in a unit that can 1) provide the appropriate segregation of duties and 2) will take the task seriously and handle it in a timely manner.

The other task that sometimes gets moved out of accounts payable is that thankless job of getting manual signature put on checks, if that is required. This is a task that most accounts payable departments are only too happy to have someone else take on.

Unclaimed property reporting, check printing, issuance of 1099s are other tasks that also get moved, if needed.

The Future

Regrettably, as long as everyone isn't 100% honest in the workplace, segregation of duties will be an issue all are forced to deal with on a regular basis. This could become a challenge as companies automate their accounts payable function, start making electronic payments in serious numbers and continue to implement process improvements that make the entire accounts payable function more efficient. These very positive actions will result in smaller more proficient staffs.

And therein lies the problem. While smaller more efficient staffs are something just about every organization desires the end result may cause a segregation of duties problem. This is not to say that readers shouldn't try to make process improvements. They should. But it also means they need to be cognizant of the fact that there could be segregation of duties issues down the road. It wouldn't hurt to start thinking now of how you'd like to solve those dilemmas.

The accounts payable world is definitely evolving and with those changes comes challenging and interesting new conundrums. Are you ready to solve them?

Control Breakdowns Created by Inappropriate Segregation of Duties

One of the principles related to strong internal controls is the appropriate segregation or separation of duties. When it comes to the procure-to-pay cycle, this means that no one person should have the ability to perform more than one piece of the transaction. By restricting this access it becomes more difficult for an employee to defraud the organization. Typically, collusion makes a fraud easier to commit. With the same person handling two or more legs of a transaction, the collusion is a done deal. What follows is a look at the different pieces of the procure-to-pay function. This is followed by identifying ten situations ripe with conflict of interest and weakened internal controls.

Dissecting the Procure-to-Pay Process

Typically there are three distinct departments involved in the procure-to-pay operation of any company. They are the purchasing department, the receiving department and the accounts payable department. Rarely do the responsibilities handled in one department overlap into a second. However, organizations with smaller accounts payable or purchasing functions may sometimes find themselves stretched to assign tasks in such a way that there are no segregation of duties issues.

Before we look at some of the potential problems that might arise if duties aren't separated appropriately, let's take a look at the different steps along the procure-to-pay trail. Most companies have different parties handling each of the following:

1. Ordering goods

2. Approving purchases

3. Receiving ordered materials

4. Approving invoices for payment

5. Processing invoices

6. Handling preprinted check stock

7. Signing checks/releasing ACH payments

8. Setting up vendors/change vendor information in the Master Vendor File

9. Handling Unclaimed Property reporting

10. Reviewing and reconciling financial records including bank recs

Where Controls Break Down

When two or more legs of the transaction are handled by the same person, there can be a problem. Now, for example, if an organization had one individual ordering goods and doing the unclaimed property reporting, there wouldn't be much of an issue. The problem is the skillset needed to do those two tasks are so disparate that no organization would have the same person performing them. The problem occurs with tasks that are in the same chain. Let's take a look at what can go wrong when certain responsibilities are handled by the same individual.

Potential Conflict #1: If the same person orders goods and then approves the purchases, there is no control and no checks and balances. Of course, the person who ordered the goods might have to review the purchase to ensure what is on the invoice is what was ordered and not something different.

Potential Conflict #2: If the same individual orders and receives purchases, there is no control over whether the goods were actually ordered in the first place. All an employee who wanted to defraud the company would have to do would be to send an invoice and claim it had been received. Alternatively, low-quality goods could be ordered while the invoice might reflect the price of much higher priced materials.

Potential Conflict #3: If the same person received goods and approved invoices for payment there would be no controls over the pricing or quality.

Potential Conflict #4: If the same individual approved purchases and set up vendors in master vendor file, it would be very easy to set up a phony vendor and submit a fraudulent invoice for goods that do not go through the companies receiving channel.

Potential conflict: #5: If the same individual could approve invoices and process invoices, there would be no controls in place to ensure the invoice was legitimate to start with. The crook would submit and approve a phony invoice and then the processor would run it through allegedly verifying it.

Potential conflict #6: By allowing the same person to process invoices and set up vendors in the master vendor file you open the door to someone setting up a phony vendor in the master vendor file and then processing an invoice against it as though it had been approved by a purchaser.

Potential conflict #7: Permitting one person to both process invoices and sign checks or release ACH payments, you are removing the checks and balances put in place to prevent an employee from processing a phony invoice or sending it to the wrong address.

Potential conflict #8: If one individual can approve invoices and set up vendors in the master vendor file, they can set up a phony vendor, submit a phony invoice and then approve it for payment. When the approved invoice shows up in accounts payable, the processor won't really know they are handling a fraudulent invoice and it will fly through your process – especially if it is for a non-PO item.

Potential conflict #9: if the same person handles preprinted check stock and sign checks, they are effectively set up with a blank company check.

Potential conflict #10: If the same person reconciles the bank account statements and handle unclaimed property reporting, they will know which checks haven't cleared. This will enable them to easily adjust the records so when the unclaimed property is turned over to the state, it is reported in their name instead of the rightful owner's name. The company's records will balance and unless the rightful owner comes forward (unlikely) the employee will claim the money that did not belong to them and no one will be the wiser.

Inappropriate segregation of duties is one sign of weak internal controls. We've uncovered ten of them above but you can probably come up with a lot more. Now, some organizations just don't have enough people working in accounts payable and purchasing to implement all the separations discussed above. They have two options.

1) Enlist employees in other departments to handle some of the responsibilities discussed. It is not uncommon to find master vendor file, bank reconciliations and/or unclaimed property handled in another department so the appropriate segregation of duties is maintained.

2) If help is not available from other departments, it is sometimes necessary to add additional steps in the process to make up for the weakened controls. This might be the president or CFO reviewing all checks before they are released in a smaller company.

The important issue is that an organization recognizes where there potential weaknesses are and create additional reviews around them.

CHAPTER 18
ENHANCING PRODUCTIVITY IN ACCOUNTS PAYABLE: THE ONGOING CHALLENGE

This chapter could probably easily turn into a book, but that won't happen here. This chapter will focus on recommendations that can be used by every organization to fine-tune their accounts payable function. Without a doubt, most organizations are probably already doing many of the tactics suggested, but there's always room for a little more efficiency. In this section we'll discuss:

- Productivity Quick Tips for Efficiency
- No-Cost Productivity Tips
- Productivity Tips to Improve the Bottom Line
- Going Paperless without a Budget Productivity Tips
- The Often-Overlooked Human Factor

Productivity Tips: Simple Ways to a More Efficient AP

Given the relentless pressure most accounts payable departments experience to be more efficient with the same size or perhaps even a smaller staff, anything that eliminates work from the accounts payable process is welcome. We've identified a baker's dozen tactics any organization can use to do just that. Let's take a look at them. Many of these will be discussed in greater detail later in this work.

- **Tactic #1** Develop a strong rigid coding standard for entering data. This includes entering information into the master vendor file, entering invoice data and creating invoice numbers for invoices without invoice numbers – if you accept them. Data entry is one place where creativity should be discouraged. Once you've got your coding standard it is imperative that everyone use it, if you want to reap the maximum benefit.

- **Tactic #2** Do not accept invoices missing a PO or the name of requisistioner. These are sometimes referred to as "invoices addressed to no one." Occasionally they are fraudulent invoices. Much time is wasted trying to figure out who initiated the order associated with the invoice. A better approach is to develop a very polite letter explaining that in order to get the vendor paid in a timely manner, invoices must contain a PO or name of the requisitioner. Return the invoice to the vendor with a copy of your letter attached. Some organizations take the same approach with invoices missing an invoice number.

- **Tactic # 3** Centralize the receipt of invoices, ideally in accounts payable. This is an issue that provokes heated discussions in some organizations when purchasing insists on getting the invoices first. Some accounts payable professionals prefer that invoices go first to purchasing as it saves them the work of either copying scanning or forwarding the invoice for approval. But, this approach is very short sighted. While it save work in accounts payable on the front-end, it creates more work throughout the process. If every purchaser reviewed invoices immediately, approved them and sent them off to accounts payable, there would be minimal problems. However, in the world most of us live, that simply does not happen all the time. When the where's-my-money calls start, the inefficiency in the process is highlighted.

- **Tactic #4** Eliminate as many paper checks as possible. They are expensive and require quite a bit of manual intervention. By converting as many vendors to electronic payments, the costs and inefficiencies associated with paper checks are reduced.

- **Tactic #5** Use p-cards to pay small dollar invoices. In fact, encourage/require the use of p-cards for small dollar items. Small dollar invoices are almost as big a productivity sapper as paper checks. Investing the precious time of your processors to handle small dollar invoices is not seeing the big picture. P-cards are the perfect solution. An effective p-card program structured to take full advantage of all the benefits the cards have to offer is a great way to get rid of all those small dollar invoices. With those gone, the processing staff can give their full attention to the higher dollar invoices which both deserve and require additional attention.

- **Tactic #6** Minimize the number of Rush payments. There are a variety of tactics to do this. Periodically AP Now runs articles detailing them. Probably the best way to minimize the disruptive interruptions associated with requests for Rush payments is to combine two tactics. Publish your check production schedule so everyone knows what is expected while making it difficult to get the payment. For example, you might require a sign-off from a senior level executive.

- **Tactic #7** Make all Rush payments using ACH. Whether you are successful in reducing the number of Rush items or not, insist that those you do make are done electronically. Completely eliminate paper checks as a payment possibility for off-cycle payments. It's one more way to reduce the number of paper checks.

- **Tactic #8** Insist on ACH for all travel and entertainment reimbursements. In most states you cannot mandate the use of ACH for payroll but you can for travel. So, take full advantage and despite the complaints from a few employees, make all reimbursements using ACH and make that process mandatory.

- **Tactic #9** Consider using per-diems for travel and entertainment expenditures. This simplifies the expense reimbursement process and eliminates a lot of the games that go on with travel and entertainment. If you do go down this recommended route, make sure you use the GSA guidelines or something lower. Otherwise, you will create a tax nightmare for both the organization and your employees.

- **Tactic #10** Use the IRS TIN Matching program to verify all taxpayer identification number information provided by your suppliers. While this may be a little more work up-front, it is another example of taking a few extra steps on the front end, to save massive headaches down the road. Organizations that use the nifty program report they almost completely eliminate those dreadful B-Notices that eat up lots of staffers' time. And, when the IRS sends notices, you cannot backburner the issue for a later date when it would be more convenient. They must be addressed immediately.

- **Tactic #11** Third party payment audits make the accounts payable function inherently more efficient in two ways. We should point out you can do an audit yourself to find the 'low hanging fruit' before calling the third party payment audit firm to find duplicate and other erroneous payments. While that is a recommended tactic there is a potential pitfall. Often organizations intend to hire an audit firm but hold off until they can do a preliminary audit themselves.

  Unfortunately, the work load and unexpected emergencies prevent the organization from ever performing that preliminary audit themself. So if you intend to do one, be completely honest – and if the task keeps getting put off, bite the bullet and hire the audit firm. The primary benefit comes from the funds they recover for you. But, the secondary benefit is often even more valuable than the money. The audit firm should provide you with a report detailing the weaknesses in your processes that allowed the duplicate and erroneous payments in the first place. Take their report and use it to plug the holes so you don't make incorrect payments for the same reason again. If the audit firm doesn't offer a management report, you might want to consider using a different firm.

- **Tactic #12** Get rid of the petty cash box. More organizations than you might imagine still have petty cash boxes. Not only do they waste huge amounts of time (paying the expenses, reconciling the box and reimbursing the box) they are an invitation to fraud. Even when fraud is not an issue, the boxes inevitably get out of balance – and rarely is that out-of-balance situation one where there is more money in the box than you think there should be. With the advent of p-cards and travel cards there is really no reason to have the petty cash box.

- **Tactic #13** Along the same lines, if you are still providing your travelers with cash advances, consider eliminating the practice, especially if you provide company credit cards. They are another productivity waster, they tend to encourage employees to be tardy with their expense reports and in a few instances encourage creative expense reporting when the employee does not wish to return the excess advance.

Simple No-Cost Accounts Payable Productivity Enhancers

Are you putting $20 worth of effort into paying $10 (or less) bills? Does your organization have processes in place that just might be a tad too robust given your strong internal controls throughout your procedures? Are you looking for ways to make your accounts payable function more efficient without spending a dime? What follows are ten simple strategies every organization can use, and they don't cost a cent to implement. You'll notice none rely on technology. So, why not cut the fat and see if you can incorporate all of the following into your routines.

1. If you are getting manual signatures on large checks, consider raising the threshold where second signatures are required. This works especially well if your signers never find errors when they review the checks before signing. By the way, if they are returning more than the occasional check, you probably need to take a look at

your up-front processes. They appear to need some improvements.

2. If you are still getting approvals on invoices that have a purchase order associated with them, consider eliminating that approval process if there are no discrepancies when you do the three-way match. For this to work, purchasers need to take great care when preparing POs in the first place – something they should be doing anyway.

3. If you have not already started reimbursing the cost of small items purchased by the staff with travel and entertainment expense reimbursements, implement a policy to do so. This will eliminate some of the small dollar invoices flowing through accounts payable.

4. Review all the reports the accounts payable department is producing and verify that they are being used. Too often, reports that were once useful are no longer used as management gets information elsewhere. Eliminate those that are not being used and look for ways to combine two into one, if much the same information is included in both.

5. If you still have a petty cash box, get rid of it. Not only is a petty cash box an incredible time waster, it creates problems. With the advances in the payment world, T&E cards, corporate procurement cards etc. there is no reason for 99+% of all organizations to have one of these productivity busters.

6. Return any invoice that does not contain a PO number or the name of the purchaser. Prepare a simple, polite letter to accompany the returned invoice stating that "in order to pay vendors in a timely manner, your organization requires all invoices to have the name of the purchaser and/or your PO number.

7. Implement a policy of NEVER returning checks to requisitioners. Not only does returning checks waste a lot of time for the accounts payable staff, it is a weak internal control. If you haven't done this already, consider implementing this strategy immediately. If you get any pushback, enlist the help of your auditors to explain why returning checks is such a weak internal control.

8. Aggressively pursue a strategy of paying vendors and anyone else you make payments to electronically using the ACH. Not only are ACH payments cheaper than paper checks, you eliminate much of the non-value add work associated with issuing checks. Best of all, you virtually eliminate unclaimed property obligations and the due diligence required by the states with regard to un-cashed checks.

9. If you are checking every detail and every receipt on your employees' expense reimbursement reports, you are spending too much time on the process, given the dollar amount of most expense reports. Gradually move to a system of spot checking, but keep checking completely those reports submitted by known envelope pushers.

10. Take a long hard look at the number of Rush checks you're handling and find ways to reduce, if not eliminate the number. This may be the biggest waste of accounts payable's valuable time. By doing everything possible to get rid of these time wasters, you'll go a long way not only to making the department more efficient but also to eliminating a constant source of aggravation for the staff.

Some of these have been discussed before in this newsletter and elsewhere so there's a good chance you are already doing some of them. With a little luck, you'll quickly implement them all taking a giant step towards having the most efficient accounts payable function possible.

Process Improvement Quick Tips that Make an Impact on the Bottom Line

Let's face it; for the most part accounts payable is a cost center. There's no way around it. Accounts payable does not generate profits for the organization. However, there are a few ways that accounts payable can have a positive impact on the organization's profitability. Let's take a look at five such strategies.

1. Aggressively pursue all early payment discounts. This does not mean take discounts regardless of when the

payment is made but rather adjust procedures so all early payment discounts can be honestly earned and taken. This might mean setting up special expedited processing for all invoices with discounts or it might mean reengineering the process so all invoices are entered immediately and scheduled for payment. Finally, and this is an important consideration, it might also include a move to electronic invoicing, thus eliminating manual delays.

2. Institute a program to regularly review statements and collect open vendor credits. Very few vendors will alert you to the fact that they have open credits for your organization on their books. Set up a program to regularly request statements and pursue your credits. The old practice of requesting statements once a year might not be sufficient. A quarterly review is likely to work better. If you don't have the necessary staff to complete this task effectively, consider hiring a third party working on a contingency basis.

3. Employ a similar strategy in looking for duplicate and other erroneous payments. Look for the low-hanging fruit yourself first and when you've found everything you can, hire a payment audit firm to look for the rest. Many work on a contingency basis, which is an especially attractive option for those who believe they don't have many duplicate payments as well as those who do not have budget for this purpose.

4. Minimize the amount of unclaimed property you have to turn over to the state. Most experts believe a large percentage of what is turned over is not really unclaimed property but rather accounting and other errors in accounts payable. The first step towards minimizing your exposure can be had by converting as many of your vendors to ACH or p-cards as possible. Regardless of how hard you try, you won't get all your vendors converted. The next step is to rigorously investigate all un-cashed checks on a very regular basis. Most organizations follow up at 90 days although some do it in one fell swoop at the end of the year. Follow up at 90 days or better yet 60 days. It will be easier to find

the vendor and sort the matter out, sooner rather than later. And, don't forget to keep all your documentation.

5. Let your employees know that your organization means to enforce its Travel & Entertainment policy, no exceptions. When an employee spends more than the policy allows that money comes right off the bottom line reducing the organization's profit. What's more, once one employee does it successfully, others feel entitled to follow in his/her footsteps. For this to work there can be no special cases. Ideally, the T&E policy should have a cover letter on it stating the organization is adopting a policy of zero tolerance when it comes to policy violations, ethical violations and fraud. It may sound tough, but it is necessary if you are to have 100% compliance.

There aren't many ways accounts payable can improve the organization's bottom line. These five tactics will allow it to do just that. Unfortunately, there is no line item that reads "Contribution from accounts payable" but if you keep management in the loop, they'll know all about your accomplishments.

Going Paperless without a Budget Productivity Tips

If you are like most people affiliated with the accounts payable function, you'd probably do almost anything to get rid of the mountains of paper. Not only does it make the office a bit more orderly, it makes the accounts payable function more efficient. If you are lucky, you work for a company that actually has budget to do just that *and* has spent it on that process. Alas, many of the rest of us can only dream of such an existence. But this does not have to be.

Lack of budget does not mean you have to completely forgo the benefits and efficiency of an electronic accounts payable department. Let's take a look at seven strategies any organization can use to get rid of some of the paper—and they don't cost a red cent.

- Start accepting invoices electronically. Typically, e-mailed invoices arrive in the form of a PDF attachment. If you print the attachment, you're not getting rid of much paper. So, figure out how you want to store these documents in a centralized location. Some retraining of processors might also be called for as they learn how to deal with an electronic document instead of a paper one.

- Have faxed invoices sent to an e-fax facility. This will automatically convert faxes to e-mails and you'll never have to deal with the paper. Once you have this in placed, your so-called faxed invoices can be treated exactly like e-mailed invoices.

- Make payments to vendors electronically. This will help get rid of those awful paper checks. And, not only will you get rid of some of the paper, electronic payments are cheaper than paper checks.

- Send remittance advices to vendors for e-payments via e-mail. This simple step will make a huge difference in whether or not some vendors accept payments electronically. By providing this information directly to the person handling cash applications, the problems many vendors have with electronic payments disappear. And, again, there's no paper.

- Send an e-mail with explanations of short payments to vendors, if information doesn't fit on remittance advice. The beauty of this approach is by taking the initiative you not only improve vendor relationships; you also reduce the number of calls coming into accounts payable.

- Automate your expense reporting process even if it's only e-mailing an Excel version of your expense reports for approval and then for reimbursement. Of course, if using Excel remember to lock the formulas to prevent employees from trying to play games with reimbursement requests.

- Make electronic payments (ACH) mandatory for all expense reimbursements. While many states still will not allow you to mandate electronic payments for payroll, you can do so for expense reimbursements for travel and entertainment expenses incurred on company business.

As you can see, none of the strategies proposed are difficult or require budget. They may necessitate a change in process, but that is easily managed. And once you've made these changes, don't forget to update your policy and procedures manual as well as train all affected employees.

Enhancing Productivity: The Often-Overlooked Human Factor

Whenever there's a discussion about productivity, most of the attention immediately shifts to technology and looking for ways to automate. But by taking that approach (which definitely has its plusses) an obvious issue is ignored. And that is the human factor, the value the staff can add to enhancing the efficiency of the function. Let's take a look at three of those options.

Option #1: Ask the staff for their ideas. It's really quite apparent, once you think about it for a few minutes. The staff spends its time dealing with the nitty-gritty of the accounts payable function. After doing it for some time, at least a few (and probably more) or your processors probably have some ideas on how to make the process more efficient. By periodically asking them for suggestions and carefully evaluating them, you can probably make the function more efficient, without spending a single cent.

Option #2: Consider for a moment the training provided for the staff for their existing positions. Is it adequate? Don't automatically assume it is. When was any re-training given? If you changed any of your processes in the last six months, did you offer any training or did you simply send a memo to everyone alerting to the change? If you took the memo route you might be surprised to find out how many of your processors are not handling the task the way you intended, simply because they misunderstood what you wrote.

Option #3: How many of the people currently on staff could take on additional tasks, including some at a higher level of responsibility? Too often, managers don't consider their existing staff when making decisions about additional work. Truth be told, thanks to technology some jobs no longer take as long as they used to. This is good news for those trying to manage the accounts payable function as they are increasingly being asked to do more on the regulatory front. What's more, there are many employees currently on your staff who could do more, if they were only asked. Some are too timid to ask and it doesn't occur to others.

When was the last time you took a good hard look at your staff to see who might be capable of handling higher-level work? And if you are a staffer reading this, when was the last time you indicated to your manager that you were interested in taking on more, higher-level tasks? This overlooked option is unfortunate from both a morale and bottom line perspective. Inevitably, there is some grousing when an outsider is brought in at a higher level. Additionally, promoting from within typically costs less than hiring from the outside. Not only is the salary usually lower, but the training and acclimation time is considerable lower.

CHAPTER 19
ENHANCING PAYMENT PRODUCTIVITY: THE ELECTRONIC PAYMENT CHALLENGE

Checks are inefficient, costly and prone to fraud. We're not only talking about the obvious expenses, the cost of purchasing check and the postage used to mail it but the salaries of your employees who must spend their days producing, verifying, mailing, and reconciling checks as well as the myriad of other tasks related to the check production cycle.

The process of producing checks is people intensive, employees who no matter how conscientious and hard-working they are, will occasionally introduce errors into the process. Errors add more cost to the process as it now takes more human intervention to fix those problems. What's more, check fraud continues to be a huge problem. Incorporating the required procedures into the mix to prevent check fraud adds more cost to the equation.

Even the issue of mailing checks becomes complicated. They must be taken to the mailroom right before the mail is delivered to the post office. If taken earlier, the company is opening itself up to the possibility that their checks will be stolen. And, if the checks don't go to the mailroom until the end of the day, where and how they are kept before that becomes an issue—again introducing more elaborate procedures (and therefore additional costs) into the check production process.

The obvious solution to the issues discussed above is to make payments electronically. In this section we'll investigate:

- Starting an Electronic Payments Program
- How to Get Suppliers to Sign up
- How to Expand Your Electronic Payments Program
- Common Problems to Avoid

Starting an Electronic Payment Program

Electronic payments are made through the Automated Clearinghouse. Hence they are frequently referred to as ACH payments. In growing numbers organizations everywhere are looking at ACH as a way to make their payment process more efficient. What follows is a plan that can be used by both those looking to get started as well as those who've taken a few tentative steps in the ACH payment arena.

Laying the Groundwork

Whether you're just beginning your investigation or have been paying a few vendors electronically, it is critical that you know what your bank capabilities are in this area. It is also important that you know what they require as well as what fraud detection and prevention services they offer. If you have them in for a meeting, it might be a good idea to also find out about their plans for the future in these areas.

Once you've got your banking facts in order, you will need to make the case to management. This includes, listing the benefits doing a financial analysis showing the cost savings as well as presenting what's available from the banking community.

You might also include any pitfalls you anticipate. This is critical because without a doubt, the process won't go smoothly. So make sure you include how you plan to address these potential issues. Then when they occur, everyone will be prepared. The problems might include:

1) Pushback from staff who are used to do everything a certain way and will have to learn a new way.

2) The impact on cash flow when all payments hit on the first day instead of being spread out over a week or so. You can renegotiate payment terms to address this issue and make it cash flow neutral.

3) Initially, you will not be able to reduce staff associated with the payment function as the personnel who normally handled your paper checks will be busy working to get vendors set up on your new payment program. Eventually you will be able to shift personnel to more value added work.

Not only do you need to convince management to convert as many payments to ACH as possibly, ideally you want to get at least one executive onboard in a big way. That way, when those inevitable complaints start appearing, you'll have someone in your corner to insist that the program move forward.

The First Date

Expect that the first few times you pay electronically it will go less than smoothly. This is normal. You need to try the program to work out whatever unexpected kinks there are in the process. If you are lucky, they will be minor. But don't hold your breathe. Assume the worst and that way you'll either be pleasantly surprised or at least not disappointed.

Given your low expectations you will want to select your test group carefully. Do not include the vendor who complains about everything no matter how much they insist. Rather choose a few vendors who are easy to work with. You might include vendors who have requested electronic payments or those who you have captive relationships with, for example subsidiaries. Practice on friends and family, so to speak, before taking your show on the road.

After your first set of transactions, review what happened and identify any problems or rough spots. Reengineer your procedures to address these complications before your second set of transactions. Only when you are certain that the process is running smoothly are you ready to roll out your program to a larger audience.

The Big Rollout

Once you've gotten your feet wet and ironed out any problems in your program, you are ready to introduce your new payment program to your vendor community. You probably want to proceed piecemeal because it does take some time to enroll each vendor. One company ended up with egg on its face after sending a solicitation to all its vendors. It got a much higher response than expected and could not get everyone on board quickly. This resulted in disgruntled vendors which was not the response they were hoping for.

A better approach might be to send a solicitation to about one-quarter of your vendors. This might include anyone who has asked about electronic payments as well as those who are sending their invoices to you electronically. These groups will probably be most receptive.

Once you've enrolled everyone from the group that shows interest, approach another group of vendors. Based on the response rate from the first group, you'll be able to figure out how big your second solicitation should be.

After each group, review the process and identify any new problems that may have cropped up. Ideally there will be none, but that is not a safe assumption.

The Hardcore Holdouts

Eventually you will have approached all your vendors. However, there will still be some who have not taken advantage of your offer, no matter how attractive it is. At that point a corporate decision needs to be made regarding how hard to push this issue.

Some organizations accept the fact that not everyone wishes to be paid electronically. Others push the issue. For example, Social Security is mandating a move to electronic payments.

Other organizations have decreased the frequency of their check runs while increasing the frequency they make ACH payments to encourage vendors to take payments electronically.

The Remittance Information

One of the reasons some companies are reluctant to accept electronic payments is their ability to apply cash. Without the remittance information that typically accompanies a paper check, they are hard pressed to apply cash correctly. You can address this concern. The simplest solution is to email the appropriate Accounts Receivable person at the vendor with the information that would typically go on the remittance advice.

Talk to your IT folks to see if they can help you devise a solution to this issue. You might also want to discuss it with your bankers when you have that preliminary meeting with them. They may be able to share with you how some of their other customers addressed this problem.

Don't Rest on Your Laurels

Once you've got the program up and running smoothly, don't rest. Stay on top of advancements in the payment arena to identify ways to improve your current process. Also, make sure you continue to monitor the fraud situation both to understand both the new frauds occurring as well as the tools being developed by the financial community to fight those scams.

And finally, don't forget to periodically calculate the savings your electronic payment program is delivering to the organization. This is money that goes right to the bottom line. Make sure management is aware of this contribution made by an improvement to the accounts payable process.

How to Convince More Suppliers to Sign up for ACH Payments

The reasons for switching from paper checks to ACH payments are many. Cost, efficiency, minimization of unclaimed property issues and cash flow planning are just a few. Despite the recognized benefits to both parties, there is still some reluctance by many suppliers to accept electronic payments. We recently asked readers of our weekly e-zine who've been successful getting vendors to sign up for ACH how they persuaded them to do so. Here's a few of the better suggestions.

The Payment Frequency Issue

Perhaps the best way to get vendors on board is to pay less frequently with checks than with ACH. That's the strategy used by quite a few of our readers. Here are a few of their comments on implementing this tactic.

- To encourage ACH, checks were cut only twice monthly whereas we did ACH daily.

- Have quicker payment terms for those vendors that accept ACH payments.

- We encourage our vendors to give us a discount and be paid by ACH. We pay these vendors on a daily basis. Otherwise, they are paid once per week.

The Benefits Approach

Quite a few companies convince vendors by simply pointing out the benefits. Here's how a few of AP Now's readers addressed the issue.

- We just let them know that by accepting ACH payments, they get paid faster and with more accuracy. No more checks lost in the mail, having to void and re-issue checks, no more phone calls from vendors looking for check payments and being told they are in the mail. ACH are easier to provide proof of payment and to validate taking early pay discounts.

- We have stressed that the time it will take for the vendor to actually receive funds will be decreased by at least a week. This is a combination of the time it takes for the checks to reach the recipient by mail, the time it takes the recipient to get the check deposited and the time it takes the bank to clear the check and make good funds available to the recipient. If an ACH is sent instead, they will have funds in their account within two business days, possibly sooner.

- We were struck by a major tornado last April. Our facilities were not impacted but unfortunately several of our vendors' physical locations were. In addition to that, during the days after the tornado, mail service was slow, if available at all in some locations. Fortunately, many of our vendors had previously signed up for ACH and we were able to continue making payments to them during this difficult time. We have been able to use this as a "plus" for ACH to convince vendors who were not signed up for ACH to do so.

The Lost Checks Opportunity

A number of readers took advantage of checks lost either in the mail or by vendors to press for ACH. Here's a look at how a few of them handle the matter.

- We charge a replacement fee for lost checks unless the vendor has submitted an ACH request for future checks.

- Whenever a vendor calls to have a check voided and re-issued, we send them a form to sign up for ACH.

- Our company doesn't replace lost checks unless the vendor submits an ACH request.

A Helping Hand from Purchasing

Increasingly accounts payable's activities overlap with other departments, especially purchasing. Here's how two of our readers recruited other departments to help.

- We encouraged the purchasing department, travel, premises or anyone engaging vendors to put ACH on the table as part of their negotiations. We managed to get some nice discount terms in the bargain.

- One of the strategies that our AP department implemented involves working in conjunction with our contracting team so that when it is time to renew our vendor price agreements, switching to electronic payment is part of the new contract.

Addressing the Remittance Information Issue

One of the biggest problems with getting vendors on board with electronic payments has to do with getting them the remittance information. Here's how two of our readers addressed that problem.

- Our company has a website where all the payments are posted (for a 3 year time frame) and the website also sends an auto email when the vendor has received a payment.

- Ask for an email address where remittance information can be sent.

Additional Strategies

Even after everything discussed, there are still a few more approaches being used by our readers. The first addresses vendor complaints about early discount payments received after the discount date and the second addresses the issue with new vendors. Here are the last two suggestions.

- We have some discount vendors still receiving checks. They will contact us requesting a discount be paid back because the check was not received in time. Our comment to this is we have no control over the mail time and suggest they switch to ACH. Allowing us to pay them by ACH they will receive our payments quicker and we will no longer have a late payment issue with discounts.

- Create a form that you can email over to all new vendors with their w9. Readers should verify information received on this form using contact information provided by the vendor.

Paying via the ACH is the wave of the future. It is much easier and less costly than paper checks. If you are looking for ways to increase participation (or get started) some of our proven reader tactics may be just what you need.

Expanding Your Electronic Payment Program

Paper checks are costly, inefficient, and a huge headaches for those toiling away in accounts payable. Yet they remain the tool used to pay the majority of invoices, even at many organizations with the ability to pay electronically. To change this situation, it may be necessary to go on the offensive and find ways to grow your ACH program. It's certainly worth the effort, given the nuisance of paper checks. What follows are seven assertive techniques to grow an ACH program be it one that is languishing or one that's thriving but could use a little extra oomph.

1. Don't overlook your password protected vendor portal on the Internet. Publish ACH information on the company Web site. Occasionally a vendor you might not have approached will want to participate. Make it easy. Also, if you are going to take this approach, include your vendor enrollment form on the site. Do this only if you are willing to include all vendors in the program. Otherwise, you may find your p-card vendors signing up for the program—and there goes your rebate. Note: If this part of your site is not password protected and accessible only by your existing vendors, do not post your information. It will only help crooks looking to defraud your organization.

2. Use a vendor satisfaction survey. Include a question in your survey asking if the supplier would like to be paid electronically. Of course, do this only if you want to include that vendor in your program.

3. Take advantage of those annoying "where's my money?" calls. When the vendor calls for timely payment assurances, point out the benefits of receiving payments electronically and try to sign them up.

4. Stop issuing rush checks. Insist that all rush payments be made using the ACH. Sometimes it just takes one payment to convert a vendor. When they see how easy it is to get paid, they may decide to sign on.

5. Use your internal e-mail to promote the program. Take a page from the marketers' book. Develop a tag line for the e-mail messages you send vendors. It could say something like "Interested in receiving your payments from us faster? Ask me about our electronic payment program."

6. Try cold calling. Don't overlook the phone as a potential tool. Make sure you target the right person. Often the pitches go to the salesperson, who in many cases has little interest in the payment aspects of the transaction.

Take your list of targeted vendors and start calling their accounts receivable or credit manager. These are the people most likely to be interested in receiving payments electronically. If you're making the pitch on the basis of financial savings, you could also try the chief financial officer, controller, or treasurer.

Overcoming Problems: Anticipate These ACH 'Gotchas' for Electronic Payment Success

Speeding up cash disbursements isn't an approach most organizations willingly adopt. It's even worse when the move is unexpected—something that somehow never happens when the organization is flush with cash. (It always seems to occur when cash is tight.) Yet, that is exactly what can happen when an organization moves from checks to ACH if they don't plan ahead and make the appropriate changes in payment terms. Whenever an organization makes a change in procedures, it is crucial that thought be given to all the ramifications; the move to ACH is no exception. We recently asked readers of our ezine who've made the move to ACH what issues others should expect so they can avoid fallout.

Extinguishing POs and Receivers

One of the first issues that come to mind is a surprising metric. While most checks payments are made through accounts payable, the same cannot be said for ACH payments. In a good number of organizations ACH payments are also initiated in other departments.

A very real concern is that the other departments might not extinguish the POs and open receivers opening the organization to another potential avenue for duplicate payments. We believe if others are to make ACH payments, it's crucial that adequate training be provided to those individuals. Open POs and receivers can result in duplicate payments should a second invoice be presented.

Additionally, state auditors could construe the open receiver as unclaimed property. And, if you think this is something I'm making up, let me warn you that a few organizations are fighting with state auditors over this very issue right now.

Should the auditors win, they will be looking at every organization's open receivers when they come for an audit.

Open receivers can cause a misstatement of your financial records if those receivers are used for accrual purposes. If there are enough of them, the misstatement could be material. This is something no one wants hanging over them.

Obviously these issues are avoided if the organization insists that ACH payments must flow through the accounts payable system.

Setup Time Involved

"Our ERP software for the pay cycle was setup to create ACH files from these invoices but the output was nothing like what was required from the bank," reports one AP manager. She notes that her staff spent endless hours completing the process to automate ACH payments. The company cut ACH payments for over 30 companies and all activity is now output to a file that is uploaded to its bank once a day. While the time savings once the process was in place is impressive, underestimating the time and effort needed to get the ACH process up and running can come back to haunt you.

This company was not home free once they had the process working, however. When they merged with another organization, they had to integrate their ACH payments with their new partners'. In this case the treasury department was involved and coordination became an issue.

Cash Flow Implications

Changing to ACH has a direct and immediate effect on cash flow. "ACHs clear the next day while your checks require mail time and deposit time at the bank, which could leave the funds in your account anywhere from three to ten days," points out an accounts payable/receivable manager.

One way to compensate for the immediate disbursal of funds, she says, would be to extend your payments to vendors a few days longer. So if you would normally cut a check on, say, May 16th wait until the 22nd to make the ACH payment. In fact, many organizations anticipate the cash flow impact and renegotiate terms with their vendors at the time they move to

ACH. Those who ignore this issue will have a rude awakening the first time the ACH payments hit.

Depending on how tight the cash flow is in your organization, this could be the worst problem of all and the one with the highest visibility. If the company runs out of cash and the cause of the liquidity crisis is identified as the move to ACH without an accompanying renegotiating of payment terms, the results will not be pretty. This is *not* how any employee wants to come to the attention of upper management.

The Cash App Issue

The remittance advice can be problematic since there is no check stub for the vendor to see what invoices are being paid. The accounts payable/receivable manager prints off remittance advices and e-mails them to the vendors. She notes she could mail it but the payment would arrive before the remittance advice. She also points out that when vendors don't know how to apply payments, they call. And that adds more work to the accounts payable department partially offsetting the productivity gains from going electronic.

Finally, if the remittance advice is mailed, the postage cost savings goes up in smoke.

Concluding Thoughts

Use of the ACH for payment processes can result in significant savings for the organization. However, like any new process, if the full ramifications are not explored its implementation can make the process worse rather than better. By addressing the issues discussed above, you will be well on your way to avoiding an ACH implementation debacle.

CHAPTER 20
ENHANCING THE BOTTOM LINE: WHERE AP CAN BRING IN CASH

While accounts payable productivity enhancements certainly improve the bottom line of the organization, they are difficult to quantify. There are only a few strategies accounts payable can use that are easily quantifiable. In this section we take a look at a few of them including:

- Earning all early-pay discounts
- Reclaimed unclaimed property escheated to the states
- The recovery of all vendor credits

Early Payment Discounts

Few CFOs or controllers would turn their noses up at an investment that returns 36% a year. In fact, most would actively pursue one that returned just a quarter of that. Yet, that is what thousands of organizations do when they allow inefficient processes to stand in the way of their firms earning those very attractive returns. What are we talking about? Early payment discounts.

Background

Some vendors offer a financial incentive to entice their customers to pay early. The most common enticement is the 2/10 net 30 payment terms. As most reading this are well aware, this means that although the payment is due on the 30th day, a customer can take a 2% discount if it pays before the 10th day. Any introductory finance book will walk you through the math that demonstrates that 2/10 net 30 is equivalent to a 36% rate of return; hence even 1/10 net 30 translates into an 18% rate of return. While the individual amounts may seem small, they do add up. Losing a 2% discount on a $10,000 invoice may only result in $200 not earned, but multiply that by the number of invoices processed and the amounts start to add up.

This issue becomes even more crucial for companies operating on razor thin margins as this extra return can make a huge difference in the bottom line. Yet, many organizations have such cumbersome and inefficient processes that it is impossible to get the invoice turned around in the requisite 10 days.

Now, if you are sitting there thinking that this is not a big deal for you because your organization takes that discount regardless of when the invoice is paid, you may be in for a big surprise. Many vendors are either billing you back for those unearned discounts or have increased their prices to adjust for your practice. Still others are trying to move away from the practice completely because as attractive as the financial incentives may be for you, they are equally unattractive to them.

The Timing Problem

This issue relates to when the clock starts ticking. Usually, the customer and the vendor have a different idea of when the timing starts: The customer believes that the time starts when the invoice hits the AP department, while the vendor starts counting on the date on the invoice.

Companies sometimes have a difficult time processing invoices in a timely enough manner to qualify for the early payment discount. Let's face it, 10 days isn't a lot of time when:

- Accounts payable has to receive and log in the invoice.

- A copy of the invoice must be sent to the appropriate person for approval.

- The approver has to review the invoice, approve it, and return it to accounts payable.

- The accounts payable associate has to process the invoice and schedule it for payment.

- The check has to be printed and signed in the appropriate check run, which can be as infrequent as once a week.

Thus it is imperative that good procedures be established regarding where invoices are initially sent and how much time executives have to approve invoices and return them to accounts payable for payment.

Making the Most of Your Discounts

The goal––assuming that it is financially profitable to take the discount––should be to take all discounts for which the company qualifies. Many companies stretch the early payment term for a few days and will take the discount up until, for example, the 15th day. Whatever the policy regarding taking discounts after the discount period has ended, it should be formalized and in writing.

If there is a problem getting invoices processed in 10 days, simply focus on your larger ones, where the real financial gain is. Payments––especially large ones––that involve an early payment discount should be flagged to ensure that they receive priority handling so that discounts are not lost. Returns like this are hard to find in this market!

Earn *All* of Them while Finding Additional Opportunities

Early payment discounts, as our readers are well aware, represent a goldmine for their organizations. Conversely the suppliers who offer them, mainly because it's been part of their business model for decades would love to get rid of them. While most don't go out of their way to openly sabotage your chances of earning these attractive discounts, they don't do anything to make it easier for you either. In this regard, there are two contributions accounts payable can make to their organizations' profitability. They can make sure they don't lose any discounts offered and they can search for additional vendors who offer them.

Let's take a look at some strategies that will help you be successful on both fronts.

Earning Every Discount

It's up to you to make sure you do everything possible to make sure you earn every last one of those discounts. Of course, the first step is making sure you receive those invoices as quickly as possible. Then those invoices must be processed quickly. Here's five ways to do that.

- **Tactic #1**: Set up a different PO Box for discount vendors. Of course, the invoices received in this box should be processed before others.

- **Tactic #2**: Try and convince as many of your early discount vendors to send invoices by email or fax. This way you eliminate the mail time and can add that extra two or three days to your processing time.

- **Tactic #3**: Have the invoices from early payment discount vendors flagged when they are received and then fast track them for processing AND dispute resolution.

- **Tactic #4**: If the invoices are going to purchasing first, make sure the approvers know which vendors' invoices need to be addressed immediately.

- **Tactic #5**: Track all lost early payment discounts and identify root causes for missing the discounts. Periodically review this information and categorize common reasons and reengineer your processes to eliminate them.

Finding More Discounts

Yes, you're not seeing things. We think it is possible for you to find additional discount opportunities for your organization. It won't be easy and there won't be a lot of them. But, we do believe you can find a few. Here's how.

Tactic #1: Instruct your processors to look for notice on every invoice. This includes vendors who don't normally offer you early payment discounts. Here's why. Occasionally a vendor will offer early payment discounts to a select group of customers. While you'd like to be part of that elite group, it's difficult to join if you don't know about it. Needless to say, the vendor has no interest in letting you know that some of its customers are getting early payment discounts. However, occasionally they slip up and someone inadvertently checks the box that causes the invoice to print the early payment discount terms on the invoice. Once you have it once, you should a) take it immediately and b) notify the appropriate person in purchasing so they can negotiate for it all the time in the future.

Tactic #2: If one vendor in an industry is offering discount terms, ask other vendors in same industry. While collusion on pricing and terms is a definite no-no, it is not uncommon to find all suppliers in the same industry offering very similar if not identical terms. Therefore, if one is offering, ask its competitors. This is a project accounts payable could work on with purchasing.

Tactic #3: If a vendor accepts p-cards and you don't have a program, ask for an early payment discount instead. In fact, consider trying to convert p-card vendors to early payment discount vendors. They may be amenable, especially if you are paying large invoices using the card. In fact, this could benefit both parties. Here's why. While you might be trading part of a rebate for the early payment discount, it is almost a certainty that the early payment discount is larger than your rebate. On the other side of the coin, your vendor can offer you an early payment discount that is smaller than discount fee it is paying its card processor. This is one time when the situation is really a win-win for both parties.

Early payment discounts offer a unique opportunity for all organizations. Make sure you not only earn every discount your organization is entitled to but you find those limited situations where additional ones are available.

Recovering Unclaimed Property: When It Will Help and When It Will Hurt

Unclaimed property is a two-way street. In theory, the states are only holding the funds turned over to them until their rightful owners come forward and claim them. Of course, as most readers are well aware, only a small percentage of owners ever come forward, leaving the states with a windfall.

When to Recover Your Funds

In theory every organization should not only be reporting and remitting their unclaimed property, they should also be looking for property that is owed them. This is one way accounts payable can add to the bottom line. However, before any organization takes this step, they should make sure they are currently reporting and remitting as they are supposed to. For if they aren't, they could find themselves facing a huge nightmare.

When to NOT Recover Your Funds

Increasingly, more and more of the states are checking their rosters when returning unclaimed property to organizations of any sort. They want to make sure the organization is reporting and remitting as it should. While they will return your property even if you are not reporting and remitting, your filing will trigger an audit.

The audit is never pretty. If you've never filed and never been audited, that first audit will be grueling. For starters, the states have the right to go back to your date of incorporation. If you find this startling, take heart. Most states limit their look back period to 20 years. That's right, that's not a typo, 20 years.

Now if you are thinking you dodged a bullet because you only have records going back seven years, think again. The states will happily estimate what you owe.

Best Practice Approach

The answer to this dilemma is simple. Every organization should be in compliance with all state and federal regulations and laws and this includes unclaimed property. If you are not in compliance, hire an expert in this area and get in compliance. Once you've sailed through your audit and it is finished, you can put in a claim for your unclaimed property.

Realize however, that the amount of money you are like to get back will be a small fraction of what you have to turn over – just one more reason NOT to put in a claim unless you are in compliance.

A Plan for Ensuring the Recovery of all Open Vendor Credits

Vendor credits are one of those dirty little secrets few organizations like to talk about. Vendor credits are those amounts of money that represent an overpayment and are held on the vendors' books. They arise from a myriad of reasons including, but not limited to:

- Returns
- Defective products
- Quantity discounts
- Volume rebates
- Simple overpayments and duplicate payments

What's The Problem?

When vendor credits are created most suppliers take one of the following courses of action:

1) They notify the customer, usually by issuing a credit memo or,

2) They do nothing.

If they issue a credit memo, it may or may not get to accounts payable. Often it is sent to purchasing. When that happens, the credit memo may be forwarded to accounts payable or it may be tossed in the garbage. Even if it is sent to accounts payable, more than occasionally, either nothing happens with it or the processor doesn't recognize it and treats it as an invoice. And of course, if the supplier does nothing, it is difficult for the customer to know of the credits.

At the end of the day, whatever the reason, many credits sit on the vendors' books unclaimed by their rightful owners. As year-end approaches, this can be a real problem. Here's why.

Accounts receivable professionals will attempt to "clean up" their accounts towards the end of their fiscal year. They also sometimes do this at the end of each quarter. They'll look at the open credits on an account and look for outstanding fees (think late fees that you don't pay) or unauthorized deductions (unearned early pay discounts and other deductions not approved by the vendor) and they'll clean up the books, using the open credits to eliminate the fees and deductions. They'll also use them to pay off disputed invoices. Many do this with the best of intentions. And then there are a few devious vendors who just take the open credits into miscellaneous income.

Clearly, if you don't take some actions to reclaim your open vendor credits, a good portion of them will be lost.

The Unclaimed Property Issue

Some reading this may rightly be thinking that open credits are unclaimed property and should be turned over to the states at the appropriate time. And, if you are thinking this you are 100% correct. If you are thinking that you'll just recover your organization's money when it is turned over to the states, you might want to reconsider.

For starters, as discussed above, the vendor credits have a way of evaporating. So, by the time the credits should be turned over, many have evaporated. This of course, assumes the vendor complies with unclaimed property rules. Experts estimate that only one-third of all organizations who should comply actually do. So, your open credits would have to be with an organization that reported unclaimed property and knew it was supposed to include open credits in that reporting.

And finally, there is the delicate issue trying to reclaim unclaimed property from the state, if you are not reporting yourself. Of course, everyone is urged to report and remit as is required by law. But, if your organization is not up to date on its reporting obligations, the last thing you would want to do would be to wave a red flag in front of the states by trying to recover your unclaimed property.

The reality is that in the last few years, many of the states have started checking their records when a company tries to recover property. If the company is not in compliance it is likely it will find itself scheduled for an audit. So, get in compliance before trying to recover property.

Recovering All Your Open Credits

The first move in the recovery process is to recognize this issue. The following steps should help you recover most, if not all, of your outstanding open credits.

- Review all accounts at least once a year. Begin by requesting the vendor send a statement showing all open activity. Make sure the vendor understands you want credits included. Otherwise, some may take advantage of the nasty feature in their software that allows them to suppress vendor credits when printing statements. Every account should be reviewed at least once a year, as credits are not always where you think they'd be.

- Identify those accounts with significant recoveries and schedule them for quarterly reviews. There's no sense leaving your funds sitting any longer than necessary. Quarterly reviews will help. Some even get monthly statements, if credit experience warrants it.

- Once the credits have been identified either request funds be returned or ask for a credit memo. Make sure you or your staff is on top of this issue, tracking credits requested and credits used. Some simply take the credit.

- Re-solicit those vendors who have not supplied recent statements. Just because you ask for the statements, doesn't mean all vendors will comply. Politely, but firmly, remind vendors who haven't sent copies of requested statements that you are waiting for them. Realistically though, be aware that it is unlikely you'll get 100% of the statements you request, no matter how persistent you are.

- Set up a regular schedule for requesting statements (and reviewing them) as part of your accounts payable procedures. It's not enough to request and receive the statements; the value comes in reviewing them and recovering the funds owed your organization.

- Keep track of all your recoveries, along with the reasons the credits were created in the first place. This information is critical to plugging the gaps in your processes.

- Analyze the data related to your recoveries to determine where you can tighten your processes to ensure future credits are not created. It's not enough to simply recover your open credits; you want to stop them from being created, where possible. It's probably not possible to completely eliminate them, but you can make a serious dent in them by studying the issues that lead to their creation.

- Periodically review new data to identify new places where you may have weaknesses in your processes that result in the creation of vendor credits. The analytical process is not a one-shot project but one that should be repeated every year or two to identify new problem spots.

Concluding Thoughts

This is not a simple project. It is something that needs to be done on a regular basis as these funds have a direct impact on the profitability of your organization. Don't have adequate resources to handle this task? Consider outsourcing it to a firm that specializes in statement review and recoveries.

CHAPTER 21
VENDOR RELATIONS:
AN OFTEN-OVERLOOKED ISSUE IN AP

Accounts payable can have an impact (good or bad) on vendor relations. In this section, we'll look at:

- Handling New Vendors

- Handling Existing Vendors

- Handling Vendor Calls into AP

- Taking a Customer-Service Approach to Accounts Payable

Although it may sometimes seem you are at odds with certain vendors, you both basically want the identical thing: a smooth relationship free of conflict and interrupting phone calls. As much as you dislike getting those calls, your suppliers hate making them. One of the best ways to achieve your mutual goal is to communicate your requirements to your vendors. If you are thinking, "Tell me something I don't know," answer this question. How do you communicate your requirements to your vendors? If you've worked with or in accounts payable for any amount of time, you know that getting suppliers started on the right foot is something many organizations overlook. Here's what you can do to keep your suppliers informed.

New Vendors

The Vendor Welcome Letter

One of the reasons there are so many problems is that different organizations expect different things from their vendors. Some want all invoices sent to accounts payable. Others want them sent to the person who ordered the goods. Virtually all want W-9s but many don't ask for them until year end. And the list of differences goes on. So, it really should come as no surprise to anyone when suppliers don't follow your approved policies for getting their invoices paid on time.

To avoid a lot of the normal confusion, many companies have taken to creating a vendor welcome letter. This explains exactly what is expected and what the vendor needs to do to get its invoices paid on time. It also tells them where to send the invoices for payment.

The Welcome Kit

Recognizing the value of getting the relationship off on the right foot, some organizations have taken the vendor welcome letter one step further. Knowing that suppliers need to be educated right from the start—before they have the chance to develop bad payment habits is the first step. So what should go in the packet? Here's what one company sends.

1) Instructions on what the vendor needs to do to be paid promptly.

2) A W-9;

3) A payee direct deposit authorization;

4) A new vendor data sheet (which asks for contact information in AR and sales);

5) A sales tax exemption certificate;

6) A standard blurb about your company and your company's standard payment terms;

7) Contact information for AP; and

8) Contact information for purchasing.

In reality, the first issue is really about what your organization wants. But, by couching it in terms for what the vendor will get (being paid promptly!) you will set the tone for a non-adversarial relationship.

Handling Existing Vendors: The Periodic Update

Now, you may be sitting there thinking this would be a great idea but what about the thousands of vendors already on the books with poor habits? Once a year send a letter to all vendors updating them on any changes you may have made. This can be as simple as a changed phone number, fax number, or e-mail address or just a reminder about a policy a few have been negligent about. Your first letter to the vendor base at large can resemble the new vendor welcome letter.

Hint: If you've been trying to convert vendors to electronic invoicing or to accept electronic payments, this is a good time to reiterate that request.

While vendor welcome letters won't eliminate all your supplier issues, they can make a significant dent in the problems.

Handling Key Vendors

All businesses rely on trusted vendors for critical goods and services. We spend years building those relationships and count on them to come through when needed, sometimes at a moment's notice. It's guaranteed, we think, that the folks we've worked with forever will be there forever. But what if we're wrong? What if, with no warning, that vendor goes out of business leaving you in the awkward or even frightening position of jeopardizing the very existence of your firm? What do you do?

Planning Ahead: Gathering Information

Rather than wait until it is too late, try approaching the situation the way a credit professional looks at their customers to determine if a problem with a critical vendor is looming on the horizon. To accomplish this, perform an annual financial review of your top 50 vendors and within that 50 closely monitor the financial well-being of your top ten suppliers.

How do you do this? Since you are the customer and vendors want your business they should be willing to supply all the information you need. Be aware, that if you are making your request to the 800-pound gorilla in your market, they may not readily comply. What should be requested from them includes:

1)   Financial statements covering three years (i.e., balance sheets, income statements, and statement of cash flow or annual reports.) If they are a public company request that copies of their 10-K/10-Q financial reports be forwarded to you from their investor relations department.

2)   The name and contact information of their outside accounting firm.

3)   The DUNS number for a Dun & Bradstreet report.

4)   The date they started in business.

5)   The type of firm (i.e., Incorporated, LLC, Partnership, etc.).

6)   If incorporated or an LLC, the date the entity was formed.

7)   Bank reference (i.e., bank account information, loans, etc. and account officer's name and contact information).

8)   Three trade references of firms in your industry or one similar that they have sold to including contact information.

9)   The vendor's Web site address.

10) The vendor's limits of capacity to provide needed products/services for your firm

11) Ability to meet your product or service needs without outsourcing the added workload (and if outsourced, for the top ten critical vendors, the same information provided on the main vendor should be obtained for the other firm covering the outsourced order).

12) Does the vendor use other firms to supply parts/services that could result in the slowdown or stoppage of critical parts/services to your firm? If so, for the top ten critical vendors, all details obtained on your direct vendor need to be obtained on their supplier(s).

13) If the vendor obtains parts/services that could directly impact your firm from a foreign vendor, for the top ten critical vendors, obtain the name and address of this supplier to your vendor.

14) Name and contact information of the following individuals from the vendor's firm:

- President/CEO
- CFO
- Credit manager
- Sales & marketing vice president
- Account sales manager

Planning Ahead: Using the Data

Now that you have all of this information, what do you do with it? On an annual basis a credit report and a full search for articles on your vendor from the Internet should be obtained. References should also be checked at this time and once all of this data is compiled it should be reviewed for possible "red flags." This should be done for the top 50 suppliers to your company. In addition, for those top ten suppliers, a look at their quarterly financial information with comparison to industry standards should be completed to confirm healthy financial trends and stability of the critical vendors .

For your top ten critical vendors, an annual meeting with an officer or top management person of the firm should be held in order to determine if the company is making any changes that would directly impact your firm's ability to obtain those much-needed goods or services. The person handling this meeting should not be from the sales and marketing side but rather from the accounting or credit side of the firm. If flags appear from your annual or quarterly analysis then a meeting should be arranged sooner rather than later.

Where Should the Responsibility Lie?

So, who is best equipped to perform this follow up function and analysis of the financial information supplied by the vendor? In the spirit of interdepartmental cooperation the most-suited person to perform this task is the credit manager. Rarely do credit managers obtain this much data and cooperation from one of their customers.

With this level of detail from the vendor, the credit manager should be able to analyze and monitor the status of the financial condition of the top 50 vendors as well as have access to industry data to compare the financial condition of the top ten critical vendors with their peers in the industry.

As a final precaution it is in every company's best interest to maintain other sources of critical supplies and services that can be drawn upon in times of emergencies. Looking at these firms in advance can make a switch from one critical vendor to another both less expensive and painful to a firm. The credit manager can also perform this look at other potential replacement vendors.

With these steps in place the scare of not having those much-needed parts or services from a critical vendor should be greatly reduced. Staying vigilant and alert to changes that directly impact a critical vendor can prevent these "surprises" from occurring. Finally, having a second source readily available can also easily ease the pain of transition from one critical vendor to another.

Vendor Calls into Accounts Payable

The first place that feels the effects of poor or insufficient vendor communications is the accounts payable department, specifically, the person charged with answering and researching vendor inquiries. The vast majority of these calls are from suppliers looking for funds. They usually want to know:

- Why they haven't been paid yet
- When they are going to be paid

- Why there were deductions taken on the payment they did receive.

These phone calls are disruptive and do not add value to the work produced in accounts payable. So, anything that can be done to minimize them will increase the efficiency of your accounts payable department. Additionally, as you may have already guessed, the tenor of the conversations, given the subject matter, can occasionally be less than cordial. The process of having one or more employees find payment information for vendors can be time consuming.

Improving Vendor Relations

There are a number of things accounts payable can do to improve the relationships with the organization's suppliers. They include:

- Make sure vendors know what they need to do to get their invoices paid on time. This relatively simple step in often overlooked and can lead to much needless annoyance. The easiest time to do this is when the relationship is first starting out before it has had a chance to go bad. Probably the best way to do this, as well as to ensure nothing is omitted, is in a vendor welcome letter. This starts the relationship off on the right foot, lets the vendor know you are happy to start it, and lists what has to be included on the invoice to get it paid on time. It also can include any special instructions you may have, such as where to send the invoice.

- Communicate, communicate, communicate. Let vendors know what to expect on an ongoing basis. Make sure everyone is telling vendors the same thing. This is especially important in times of tight cash and, perhaps, delayed payments. For example, the company may have decided to pay everyone in 60 days instead of the normal 30. Vendors won't be happy, but they will be a lot less upset than if they are not told when they call. Setting the policy for this communication is something that is typically outside accounts payable's area of responsibility; normally, it's a policy set by the CFO, the controller, or treasurer. The point I am trying to make here is no accounts payable manager should take this on him or herself or they may end up pounding the pavement.

- Timely dispute resolution. Usually someone in accounts payable is responsible for invoice disputes. This is something I have never understood as purchasing is typically the party with the needed information. However, the responsibility for this often-odious task lies in accounts payable in most organizations. A happy vendor is one whose disputes are settled quickly so payment can be made with as little holdup as possible. The responsibility for resolving disputes lies typically either with one person or with each processor. Make it part of your departmental goals to get these disputes settled as quickly as feasibly possible. Your vendors will be less dissatisfied and it will cause less consternation among the staff.

- Provide payment status information to your vendors. In an ideal situation this can be done online without your vendors ever having to talk to any of your processors—a win-win for everyone involved. This will result in many fewer "Where's-My-Money?" calls in your accounts payable department.

- Vendor portals with complete information. How often do you get a call from a vendor only to have to make several more yourself before you can provide the information the vendor requests—which usually is when will the supplier be paid and if there is a hold up, where it is? Wouldn't it be nice if that information were easily available online and your supplier could see that the holdup is the purchasing executive who hasn't approved the invoice for payment yet? The beauty of such a setup, at least from accounts payable's standpoint, is the vendor could then call the purchasing executive, leaving accounts payable out of the conversation completely. It also would put an end to the games where purchasing tells the vendor the invoice had been sent to accounts payable for payment weeks ago. This is the type of functionality available on vendor portals today. Be aware that organizations that install these portals, eliminating much manual work and human intervention, also typically reduce the size of the accounts payable staff.

While all these steps will strengthen the affiliation between accounts payable and the vendor, AP doesn't have the responsibility to authorize all of them. It can, however, advocate for them—and by pointing out potential vendor relationship enhancements, the odds of having them implemented are definitely better.

When a Caller to AP Flips Out: Uncovering the Real Cause

Have you ever gotten off the phone with a vendor looking for payment or an employee looking for a T&E reimbursement and wondered, *"What is his problem?"* The anger over the late payment appears to be way out of proportion – at least to you. Perhaps you were five days late or the amount of money in question is only several thousand dollars. Before jumping to the seemingly obvious conclusion that the guy is a jerk, step back a minute and consider the real impetus for the over-the-top reaction.

Once you determine the root cause for the out-of-proportion response, you can decide if and how you want to meet their requests. Let's, analyze the different types of professionals who might call accounts payable looking for money or information to determine their real underlying motivation. Here's a look at the seven types.

- **Collectors/Credit managers/AR managers**. These professionals typically call looking for past due monies. That is their job. What you may not realize is some of them have a portion of their compensation tied to a DSO (days sales outstanding) calculation. The longer it takes for the funds to come in, the lower their bonus is. They are likely to get particularly agitated at the end of a period (typically quarters) when the bonus is calculated and paid. Part of their angst may be related to the fact that your delay in payment is costing them personally.

- **Business owners with cash flow issues**. Small business owners, especially in the last few years, are particularly dependent on cash flow to meet their obligations. Often there is little room for slack or delay.

Your few days late might mean they can't meet a looming bill or worse, can't make payroll.

- **Employees with credit card bills due**. If your organization makes the employee personally responsible for the credit card bill used for company travel, a delay in reimbursing the employee could mean he or she doesn't have the funds to make their credit card payment. This can be particularly frustrating to the employee if he or she turned the expense report in on time and then the manager delayed approving it.

- **Sales people whose commission dependent on collections**. While it was a complete anomaly years ago to have commissions tied to accounts receivable, savvy companies are doing just that. This helps ensure sales are not made to organizations that can't pay their bills and it gets the sales person to help with collections. Unfortunately, at the end of a month or quarter, if collections have been slow, some sales people can get downright aggressive in trying to make sure those funds are collected. For if the money doesn't come in, their bonuses will be lower, and sometimes significantly lower. In a few rare instances, organizations will reduce the commission a sales person gets if the collections are particularly late.

- **Analysts needing data to make a presentation to management**. These individuals often have a very short timeframe, sometimes just a matter of days, to prepare their talks. It never seems to fail that their request for data comes at an equally bad time for you and the data they need is not standard. Thus, you'll need to spend some time figuring out how to coax the information from the system. You feel comfortable in promising them something in two weeks. Unfortunately their presentation is in three days.

- **Purchasing needing data to negotiate better pricing**. This is similar to the analyst situation. It can be compounded by the fact that the requests often come with a very short timeframe, either because the supplier has made an offer that needs to be acted on quickly or the purchasing executive didn't realize until the last minute that you might have the data he or she needs.

- **Crooks**. That's right; the fellow on the other end of the phone might be a thief who knows that if he rants and yells enough and threatens a credit hold, his chances for a Rush check improve dramatically.

Your mission is to:

- Figure out which type of person you have on the phone (crook or legitimate business person) and

- Decide what to do.

By understanding the underlying dynamic behind the seemingly irrational behavior, you can factor that into your decision to either issue a Rush check or tell them to wait. As regular readers are aware, we are not big proponents of Rush checks. In fact, we advocate against them.

However, there are those rare occasions when issuing one is the right thing to do. If there is a financial concern you can get double bang for your buck if you issue an ACH payment. The recipient will get the money faster and you may have converted one more vendor to electronic payments. Just make sure you employ the same stringent processing standards as you would to a normal invoice. This includes:

- Getting the invoice approved and the invoice number entered,

- Doing the three-way match and

- Extinguishing the PO and the receiver.

Don't overlook the fact that any of the individuals mentioned above may be trying to improve their payment situation and may actually be requesting money before it is due. In that case, keep in mind that your obligation is to your employer and you are not a charity.

By understanding the root cause of the outrage, you will be better situated to deal with the situation.

Taking a Customer-Service Approach to The AP Function

As much as I hate to admit this, more than a few accounts payable departments have a less-than-stellar reputation within their organization and with their vendors. This can be partially attributable to the way they interact with their "customers." Now, if you are thinking, "now wait just a minute, we're the customer," you are technically correct. In the transaction itself your organization is most definitely the customer. But we're taking a bigger picture view in this matter. In this piece we'll take a look at who we think AP's customers are, what we mean by a customer-service approach and why it is so important to treat them correctly.

Who are AP's "Customers"?

Generally speaking, accounts payable has three broad sets of customers. They are:

- Vendors calling looking for information about invoices
- Employees calling looking for information about their expense reports
- Employees calling looking for information about vendor payments

They can be viewed as customers because accounts payable provides them with a service, usually in the form of information. By treating them respectfully and getting them their information quickly, everyone benefits. This is discussed in detail below.

Don't Become a Doormat

While we emphasize getting the customer information quickly and politely, this does not mean doing whatever is asked. What it does mean however, is that information (whether it's good or bad) is provided in a timely manner. This is done within the guidelines of running an efficient accounts payable operation that incorporates strong internal controls.

Remember, at the end of the day, the accounts payable group is charged with guarding the organization's assets. So, if a vendor calls and asks (or demands) to be paid early, firmly and politely tell them no. If an employee comes running in at the last minute requesting a rush payment for a tardy expense report, the answer is also a polite no.

To address these issues it is imperative that both employees and vendors know what your requirements are. If they are educated to the cut-off schedule for check requests, the payment terms and other information affecting the payment process, these unpleasant situations are less apt to arise.

Benefits of a Customer-Service Approach

The advantages of taking this approach to dealing with those who interact with the accounts payable staff are numerous. Let's take a look at some of them.

- Improves vendor relations. For starters, if people come to expect an efficient response from the accounts payable staff, relations with vendors will get better. This won't happen overnight, but it will occur over time.

- Resolve discrepancies faster. Once relations with vendors improve, it will become easier to resolve discrepancies. If vendors don't dread talking to your staff, they will respond more quickly and will be more likely to try and resolve issues in an equitable manner, rather than taking a high-handed approach. Also, they won't be dragging along any baggage from prior encounters. As with the improvement in vendor relations, this won't happen overnight.

- Earn more early pay discounts. If you are able to resolve discrepancies quickly, you will earn more early payment discounts. Also, as your relationships with other employees in the organization improves, they too are likely to respond faster to your inquiries making it easier to earn those coveted early payment discount.

- Get fewer late fees assessed against your account. If discrepant invoices are resolved before the payment date and payment is made on time, there will be no need to assess late fees. Even though many companies don't pay late fees, many suppliers do asses them and use unclaimed vendor credits to wash them away.

- Receive fewer second invoices. Time spent handling and identifying second invoices and making sure they are not paid is time that could be spent on more value-add functions. If discrepancies are resolved quickly and invoices paid on time, the vendor won't send that dreaded second invoice.

- When operations run smoothly, there are fewer vendor complaints to deal with. That's a win-win for both customer and supplier.

- When problems are resolved quickly, there's less resources needed for that function leading to a more efficient accounts payable function. This translates directly into an improved bottom line for the organization as it spends less on resolving problems related to accounts payable. And, improved profitability benefits everyone.

- Occasionally, even the best run operations run into problems. Sometimes, in order to get those issues resolved, help is needed from the vendor. If you have a good relationship with the vendor they are going to be more apt to help and to pitch in quickly when you have a problem.

- And lastly, the reputation of some accounts payable departments leaves a lot to be desired. Whether it's the staffs fault or not is beside the point. By taking a customer service approach towards both internal and external customers, the image and stature of accounts payable department and staff will improve. Rome wasn't built in a day and repairing a tarnished reputation won't happen overnight either. However, by slowly plugging away at the issue, the department will start to be viewed in a much better light. This is just a side benefit, but a nice one.

CHAPTER 22
THE FUTURE OF THE ACCOUNTS PAYABLE FUNCTION

It seems that anything that can possibly be touched by technology is a lot different than it was just a few short years ago. So, it's really no surprise that the accounts payable function is undergoing a massive transformation, at organizations of all sizes. Let's take a look at what's been going on in the last few years and where the accounts payable function is headed. In this section:

- We'll look at changes that have occurred in the last few years
- What needed to meet the challenges of those changes
- Changes due to technology

Granular-Level Changes in The Last Few Years

For starters, the accounts payable function is no longer an island unto itself. Rarely does the department function in a silo anymore. Today it operates as an integral part of the finance and accounting chain. In some organizations, mainly those that are not heavily dependent on the procurement function for the core business, the accounts payable function and the purchasing department are run by the same person. The procure-to-pay (P2P) function is cleanly integrated and runs much more efficiently when the two arms work together towards the same goal rather than taking divergent paths.

The accounts payable function, in general, has made great strides in the area of reducing duplicate payments. While technology certainly has played a role in this arena, the professionals who work in accounts payable deserve a lot of the credit. By making some very basic changes (mainly insisting on standardization in processing and data entry) the number of straight duplicate pays has plummeted. This doesn't mean there aren't other types of inaccurate and incorrect payments, but the easy errors have been largely eliminated.

The Regulatory Component

At the same time, there have been increased regulatory pressures. These come in two forms. For starters both the states and the Federal government have been quite vocal and active in requiring better compliance with existing statutes. This means those who haven't been complying at all are now being identified (usually through painful audits) and brought into compliance. It also means that those who have been complying haphazardly and not completely are being called on the carpet, again through the painful audit process.

Then there is the issue of constant changes of existing requirements, the end result being that money is turned over more quickly (i.e. reduction in dormancy periods for unclaimed property) or rate changes (in the case of sales and use taxes).

And finally, there are new issues that are either brand new or were on the books but never enforced. The brand new issues include things like the 1099 reporting now required by some states. Both OFAC screening and FCPA have been on the books for years, but have only recently started to get visibility.

The Fraud Component

Unfortunately, fraudsters have also taken advantage of technology to further their "careers." They are using it in ways never imagined before. They understand how the banking process works. They have an intricate knowledge of computers, the Internet and security issues. And they combine all this to develop unique ways to get their hands on funds that do not belong to them.

While the banking and business community have done a fair job at developing products to combat this growing threat, continual awareness is necessary. What's more, employees often take actions which seem harmless but end up exposing the organization to increased risk from these manipulative and conniving crooks.

Implications of These Changes

For starters, it's fairly apparent that automation and technology have been key drivers in the shift that is going on in the business environment in general and in the accounts payable function in the specific. Plummeting costs have put the technology within the reach of just about every organization. The evolution first of SaaS (software as a service) and then cloud capabilities is making a massive difference in who has access from an affordability standpoint.

It also has changed the way the office can be structured. No longer is it necessary for everyone to be located at the same physical location at the same time – although that does remain the norm in most organizations.

Best practices are shifting, evolving quickly to meet the challenges presented by our changing environment. In extreme cases yesterday's best practices have become worst practices and the reverse. More commonly, new best practices are being developed to handle the multitude of new processes, procedures and experiences.

There's also been the emergence of new products and services to meet the ever-changing landscape of the accounts payable function. This is especially true in the fraud arena, where the community is faced with frauds perpetrated in manners never dreamed of in the past. These are particularly perplexing as the perpetrators are often located in other countries beyond the long reaches of the arm of the law.

A Very Different Future of Accounts Payable

The first change we've seen is the emergence of new terminology related to issues affecting the accounts payable function. One massive change we've seen and expect to continue is the emergence of vendor partners who develop specialty products to enhance the accounts payable functionality. Looking back into the not-so distant past, these products were mainly focused on travel and entertainment reporting and duplicate payment recovery. The first e-invoicing products introduced ten to fifteen years ago were on the pricey side, although to be fair some of the cost issues have gone away.

Today there is a wide array of products available to enhance the accounts payable function. The vendors offering them are quite innovative and understand the dynamics of the market. Readers are advised to study their offerings both online and at conferences and wherever possible attend online demonstrations and webinars offered usually for free by these vendors. It's a great way to learn about the latest innovations in the marketplace.

In the past, new technology innovations were often quite expensive, limiting their target audience to only the very largest companies with pockets deep enough to handle the purchase price. Largely, although not completely, the cost issue has changed. Moving forward we expect cost to be less of an issue for more of the innovative products introduced to the market.

To be honest, in the past, requirements of the accounts payable function were not always given the same attention when ERP systems were being developed. That is all changing and today most of the developers realize the importance of the accounts payable function – after all, it's the organization's money.

They are starting to incorporate some of the functionality offered by the specialty vendors in the biggest ERP offerings. We saw this with duplicate payment checking routines. This has been partially responsible for the reduction in duplicate payments.

As time goes on, expect more of these specialty functions to be offered in ERP systems. But make no mistake about it; this is one area where price will most definitely be a consideration. This functionality will not come cheaply.

That being said, for the foreseeable future, there will definitely be a place in the market for the specialty vendors offering their innovative products that help the accounts payable function run more efficiently and effectively.

There is another issue emerging that is likely to change forever the way organizations look at technology. The BYOD (Bring Your Own Device) movement is taking hold with a greater number of employees buying their own devices (smartphones and tablets) and using them for company work. Policies addressing this issue will have to be developed. A few are starting to do that.

With regards to these devices, some organizations are looking to their employees to purchase their own devices and use them for their professional responsibilities. If this approach takes hold (and there is some evidence that it has), questions about security will become paramount. And of course, there will be the issue of getting company data off personal devices should an employee separate from the organization (either voluntarily or involuntarily). Of course, if the data resides in the cloud it may simply mean cutting off access. This type of issue will be on the forefront for the next few years as companies work through the problems and develop policies.

The Role of Technology in AP Today and Tomorrow

Without a doubt, the relentless march of technology has changed the face of the accounts payable function forever. In all likelihood, it will continue to have an impact in the near future. AP Now isn't really going out on a limb predicting that the accounts payable department of 2020 will look a lot different than the function does today. In this section, we take a look at 20 different ways, technology has changed and continues to impact the way the accounts payable process is handled. While most of the change has been good, you'll note the last item on our list is a definite negative.

1. E-mail communications. Most don't even think of e-mail as a technology innovation but the reality is that it's only in the last decade or so that e-mail has become a standard tool. It helps to reduce the number of phone calls coming into the department and has generally made the staff more efficient.

2. Invoice automation. Third-party or home-grown invoice automation programs were initially very expensive. Today the price has plummeted bringing the cost within

the reach of most mid-size organizations. Moreover, many of these programs available on a pay-as-you-go basis eliminating the huge up-front investment that was often an obstacle in the past. Invoice automation often marries up-front scanning with workflow.

3. Invoices received by e-mail. PDF files now make it possible for organizations from as small as one-person companies up to the very largest to be able to e-mail their invoices to vendors. And that is exactly what is going on. In fact, some companies are refusing to put invoices in the mail claiming it is too expensive. And, they are correct. We expect the e-mail receipt of invoices to become increasingly commonplace and organizations need to adjust their processes to make sure they are ready for this change.

4. Expense reimbursement automation. Like invoice automation, the automation of expense reporting has come down in price drastically. The best of these models check for policy compliance and flag violations. They enable 100% verification without allocating headcount to this tedious task.

5. Internet self-booking of travel. No longer do most organizations book travel through a corporate travel office or a travel agent. In many organizations, employees search for the lowest fares themselves. What's more, online travel services are now offered to the corporate travel market by the companies that handle online booking. Their services are cost-effective, while offering many of the benefits of the traditional travel office.

6. Online verification of mileage. Sites such as Mapquest and other online travel planners provide the staff handling expense reports the ability to verify mileage put in by employees using their personal vehicle for company business. This functionality is being built into the some of the best next generation of expense reimbursement automation products.

7. Online language translators. These online services, usually free, help with the verification process of receipts in different languages. More than one processor

has been able to weed out an expense that was clearly personal in nature from a reimbursement request.

8. Scanned receipts. Even organizations that have not dipped their toes into the paperless waters when it comes to invoicing are moving forward having employees scan their receipts for their expense reports. They do this either using a scanner or their cell phone to take pictures of the receipt. The picture is then e-mailed either to the processor or to themselves for attachment to their expense report. Currently, most of the receipts from cell phone pictures are not of great quality, but that is expected to change over time.

9. Remittance advice delivered by e-mail. One of the biggest obstacles in getting vendors to accept electronic payments is the remittance advice needed by the professional handling cash application. Smart companies have set up processes whereby this information is e-mailed and thus eliminating the final excuse in getting the supplier to accept electronic payments.

10. Self-service portals for vendor information. By having vendors input their own data into your master vendor file, companies solve many problems. It is also easier to get contact information updated and eliminates some of the risk associated with certain types of ACH fraud. Until recently, the only companies who had such portals were the giants who built these vehicles. The cost of these projects was not unsubstantial. However, today, there are third-party models available for a fraction of the cost of developing a home-grown model.

11. Self-service portals for payment status/visibility. The ability to let the vendor check on the payment status of an invoice without calling the accounts payable department is a real plus. This capability is now available sometimes as part of the vendor portal discussed above and sometimes part of the invoice automation model. Used correctly, it greatly reduces the number of phone calls into the accounts payable department.

12. ACH payments for invoices. Most organizations have long offered their employees the ability to have their

Mary S. Schaeffer

paychecks directly deposited into their bank accounts. This same functionality can be used to pay vendors. Handled in accounts payable, not payroll, this practice eliminates a lot of the hassles associated with paper checks. It also gets rid of a lot of paper and it's a less expensive payment mechanism.

13. ACH reimbursement of expenses. While direct deposit of payroll cannot be mandated legally in most states, the same is not true for the reimbursement of travel expenses. Savvy companies do just that eliminating some of the headaches associated with using checks to reimburse employees for out-of-pocket travel expenditures.

14. IRS TIN Matching. Possibly one of the best things the IRS has ever done for business was to make available the use of the program it uses itself to verify name/TIN matches. Companies that take advantage of this free service drastically reduce, if not completely eliminate, the number of B-Notices they receive each year. This makes the accounts payable function more efficient as staff does not have to be allocated to work the B-Notices.

15. Sales and use tax payments to the states via ACH debits. While many probably do not see this as a benefit—and we can't disagree—some of the states have taken advantage of technology utilizing ACH debits to collect the sales and use tax they are owed. Still, it is one more way technology is impacting the accounts payable function.

16. Online unclaimed property listing. Just about all the states now offer online listings of the unclaimed property they are holding. Some only have recent "acquisitions" online and are working on getting back information uploaded. This allows companies to identify and claim their own property rather easily. However, any organization is cautioned against claiming their own unclaimed property if they are not currently reporting and remitting. Putting in a claim will set off a red flag and the ensuing audit will not be pretty. Better to get

your unclaimed property house in order and then put in your claim.

17. Social media in accounts payable. Most of us think of Facebook and LinkedIn as having little business value, although they may help the individual personally. Using social media to find rightful owners of unclaimed property is a lot easier than doing the due diligence required by the states. This works especially well with former employees who might not have received their last pay check or expense reimbursement. This happens frequently when an employee moves at the same time they separate from the organization.

18. Use of personal devices in accounts payable. By personal devices we mean smartphones and tablets. In growing numbers employees have been acquiring these devices themselves and then using them for company business. While on the face of it, this might seem like a generous move on the part of the employee, it could backfire. This is especially true in those instances where strong anti-virus software has not been put on the device. Each company should develop a policy on how they want this issue to be handled.

19. Job listings on LinkedIn. It was just ten years ago that LinkedIn launched the service that most people today use as the basis for their professional networking. What's more, it's the best place for companies to list their open positions and the site most go to when looking for a position. The whole concept of an online professional profile (i.e. resume) was unheard of just a few short years ago. This has changed the way we look for future employees, giving companies the opportunity to check someone out without spending a dime or calling to verify references.

20. ACH fraud via account takeovers. Unfortunately, not all the changes related to technology have been good. Without technology, we would not be dealing with the latest treacherous fraud, which comes into our offices uninvited through our computers. What this means, aside from requiring that everyone be knowledgeable not only about how it is committed but also how to protect against it, is that everyone has to keep updated

about the troubles technology can cause as well as the benefits. It's not a one way street.

The next few years will be an exciting time to work anywhere in the accounting/finance chain. For once, accounts payable will be an integral part of the evolution that is going to occur. This is not time to look for a rest. There is a great deal of change coming and this means continual learning, innovation and a lot of hard work. The end result will be greater responsibilities for a smaller staff as transactional jobs disappear and analytical positions become more the norm. The individual who can look into the future, sort through the change and pick out the innovations that will best benefit the organization and then implement those recommendations will be in high demand. Are you ready?

GLOSSARY

ACFE – Association of Certified Fraud Examiners

ACH – Automated Clearing House

ACH credit – An electronic payment initiated by the payor

ACH debit – An electronic payment initiated by the payee

B-Notice - An annual IRS notification to payers, that IRS Forms 1099 have been filed with either missing or incorrect name/TIN combinations.

BYOD – Bring Your Own Device, generally refers to smartphones and tablets, but a few include laptops in the term.

DOJ – Department of Justice

Duplicate Payment – The unintentional second payment of an invoice. One type of erroneous payment and unfortunately, rarely returned by the vendor unless the customer or its audit firm discover the over payment.

e-Invoice – An electronic invoice either provided through an automated approach or as simple attachment to an e-mail. Some do not consider files attached to e-mail as true electronic invoices.

FCPA – Foreign Corrupt Practices Act

Form 1099 – The Form 1099 is used to report different types of taxable income; the most common for the accounts payable groups being Form 1099MISC. This is used to report income paid to independent contractors.

IFO – Institute of Financial Operations

Internal Controls - The group of policies and procedures implemented within the organization to prevent intentional or unintentional misuse of funds for unauthorized purposes.

IVR – Interactive Voice Response

IWR – Interactive Web Response

MCC - Merchant Category Code

NACHA - National Automated Clearing House Association

OFAC – Office of Foreign Assets Control

P-card – Sometimes referred to as corporate procurement card or purchasing card.

Packing slip – Sometimes referred to as receiving documents, delineates exactly what was delivered in a particular shipment. Used in the three-way match.

PO – Purchase Order

Receiving documents – See packing slip.

S-Ox – Sarbanes Oxley Act

SEC – Securities and Exchange Commission

Segregation of Duties – With regards to accounts payable, it is the division of work so that one person does not perform more than one leg of the procure-to-pay function. It is one of the foundation principles of strong internal controls.

Three-way Match – Comparison of invoice with purchase order and receiving documents before payment is made. If there is a discrepancy, some investigation is required to eliminate the discrepancy before payment is made.

T&E – Travel and Entertainment

UCC – Uniform Commercial Code

W-9 – Its full name is Request for Taxpayer Identification Number and Certification and it is provided to customers who need to verify certain tax reporting information.

EXCERPT: 101 BEST PRACTICES FOR ACCCOUNTS PAYABLE

Issue: Who Has Access to the Master Vendor File

While it is definitely easier for the staff processing invoices for payment if they can add vendors to the master vendor file whenever they get an invoice from a new vendor that practice is an invitation to trouble. Unfortunately, that's how a number of organizations handle information into the master vendor file. This means giving access to the master vendor file to a large number of individuals. This is a terrible idea. It completely disregards the best practice concept inherent in all accounting functions of having appropriate segregation of duties.

Best Practice: Access to the master vendor file, for anything but information lookup, should be severely limited. Only a few people should be able to enter information, be it for setup or to make changes. The employees with this access should not perform any other tasks in the procure-to-pay function making it more difficult for someone to defraud the organization. What's more, when they go on vacation, their passwords and access should not be given to someone else. This will simply muddy the audit trail should there be a problem down the line. A better approach is to set the back-up person up with their own user ID and password and then deactivate those when the person with primary responsibility for the task returns. This is less of a problem in large organizations where there will be several people working on the master vendor file.

Almost Best Practice: This is a black and white issue so there really is no almost best practice. In many organizations there is one or two people with access to the entire accounts payable function. Typically this is the manager, director or perhaps the Controller. While this is not a good idea, it does solve the problem of an unexpected absence, assuming the person with the broad access is willing to dive in and handle the task. Really, though, unlimited access is not a good idea.

Pointer for Accounts Payable: While limiting access for the purposes of adding new vendors or updating information on existing vendors can seem to make the accounts payable function run less smoothly, it is imperative from an internal control standpoint. Sometimes what is easier for accounts payable is not necessarily good for the organization as a whole and this is one of those instances.

Worst Practices:

- Letting each processor update information about their own vendors
- Letting each processor add vendors whenever it seems necessary

INDEX

ABOUT THE AUTHOR

Mary S. Schaeffer, a nationally recognized accounts payable expert, is the author of 18 business books, a monthly newsletter and a free bi-weekly e-zine, as well as several CPE courses for CPAs and worked with the IFO to create the Innovating AP certificate program.. She runs AP Now, a boutique publishing and consulting firm focused on accounts payable issues. Before turning to writing and consulting she worked in the corporate world as an Assistant Treasurer for the Equitable Life Assurance Society, a Financial Risk Manager for O&Y and a Corporate Cash Manager for Continental Grain. A frequent and popular speaker at industry live and online events, she has an MBA in Finance and a BS in Mathematics.

About AP Now

AP Now is the leading source of accounts payable information for the business and finance community. It offers a host of products and services designed to advance your department, your company, and your career. These include:

- E-AP News weekly ezine (free)
- Accounts Payable Now & Tomorrow Newsletter (monthly fee-based publication delivered by e-mail)
- Webinars/teleconferences
- Seminars
- CDs
- Books
- Consulting services
- Customized Training (including FCPA)
- Duplicate Payment Resource Center (complimentary)

8454283R10162

Made in the USA
San Bernardino, CA
15 February 2014